SAINT JOHN OF THE CROSS

SAINT JOHN OF THE CROSS

Reflections on Mystical Experience

ALAIN CUGNO

Translated by Barbara Wall

THE SEABURY PRESS NEW YORK

To Julien

1982
The Seabury Press
815 Second Avenue
New York, N.Y. 10017

Original edition: *Saint Jean de La Croix* © Editions Fayard, Paris, 1979.

English translation © Search Press, Ltd., 1982.

Printed in the United Kingdom.

Library of Congress Cataloging in Publication Data

Cugno, Alain, 1942—
   Saint John of the Cross.
   Translation of: Saint Jean de la Croix. 1979.
   Includes bibliographical references.
   1. John of the Cross, Saint, 1542–1591.
2. Mysticism—Spain. 3. Mysticism—1450–1800.
I. Title.
BX4700.J7C8313   248.2′2′0924   81 14430
ISBN 0–8164–0132–2   AACR2

CONTENTS

AUTHOR'S
ACKNOWLEDGEMENTS

This work is largely the fruit of friendship, so it is with delight that I take the opportunity of thanking:

Claude Bruaire, professor at the University of Paris–IV, for his enthusiastic encouragement; Chantal Alcouffe, my wife, who not only translated the texts from John of the Cross but helped me as only she can; Geneviève Ginvert, who brought all her intelligence to bear on reading the manuscript and closely collaborating in its final re–working.

Without these three the book would never have been published—nor would it without the generous understanding of Robert Toussaint, so may he be warmly thanked too.

INTRODUCTION

What this Book is About . . .

Essentially it is about John of Yepes, better known by his name in religion, John of the Cross. He was a mystic, perhaps the greatest ever produced by Christianity. He was Spanish; he was born in Castile in 1542 and died in Andalusia in 1591.

It should be made clear at the outset that this book is based on a philosophical work done for the University of Tours. Hence it is primarily philosophical, not theological, and still less 'mystical.' It is not concerned exclusively with John's thought (although this will receive its fair share of attention), nor is it an initiation into mysticism, a spiritual guide–book or an attempt to teach the reader practices that supposedly bring peace or 'ecstasy' or some other yoga of the spirit. But it is concerned with John's teaching and, starting from there, with mysticism as it is understood in the Christian tradition.

Second, to say that this book is philosophical rather than theological means that it is addressed to a readership not necessarily burdened with religious belief—in other words the book is free from preconceptions and intended for everyone. John treated of basic matters, indeed his writings contain the essence of what is open to man's understanding. This needs to be stressed because the essence matters to everyone; it matters much more than distinctions between believers and non–believers, philosophers and non–philosophers, the educated and the ignorant, or any other distinction that people like to make.

Let it not be thought, however, that John did not belong to the Christian faith, or that his teaching forms part of a common inheritance and could be appropriated by any ideology. The opposite is the case—it is because John's thought was so faithful to itself and so bound up with his vision of life that it can aspire to truth and universality.

We all play our part in the same world, have the same difficulties, face the same problems—the anguish of death, love, evil, of the fact that there is being rather than nothing. But we also have to solve these problems, and for this we are all equally equipped. Metaphysical questions are not the preserve of metaphysicians any more than food is the preserve of physiologists. The metaphysician's speciality is not to answer metaphysical questions but to answer them intelligibly—which is a very different matter. As for philosophers or theologians, their only privilege (but it is a considerable one) is to know that what others experience is much more important than they themselves often suppose.

This book is the account of a man who was very well aware of what he understood and what he experienced and managed excellently well to tell others about it. And perhaps in the course of their ordinary lives, people who are not philosophers or theologians have unknowingly encountered—not what John said, but at least the tools for understanding what he said. John wrote about the realities that we all come up against. He did not deal with a world specific to himself or reserved for people who are different from the rest of us. Some passages in his writings might lead us to think that he did, but this does not present any difficulty or detract from what has been said, that John's writings are essential to each and every one of us. Misunderstandings can arise from complications of vocabulary, from false ideas current at the time, and other matters. This work is an attempt to interpret the real John.

It could be said that by and large everything John taught and wrote revolved round the problem of religion. The question vibrating in his work was the question of God, and this is why his writings lie at the heart of *every* question. For surely in a general and theoretical way nothing is more important than the question of whether God does or does not exist. All the problems already referred to (death, love, evil) are coloured according to whether God does or does not exist. Unfortunately the question is not altogether symmetrical, for it is of much greater weight if God exists than if he does not. If God exists then the question of his existence is the most important of all questions. If it is discovered that he does not exist, then the question of whether he exists is of interest but much less importance. As we can only see the backs of the cards, the question remains open. However it has to be assumed, and precisely because of its asymmetry, that the question merits investigation, and that the elements of an answer can be found by studying the works of someone who believed that God *does* exist.

John did not ask direct questions concerning God's existence. For him, a proof of God's existence was not nonsensical, but it did not matter, because he lived so closely with God. When we love people we do not ask whether they exist, or whether their existence can be proved, for it is their very existence, the fact that they simply are, that draws us to them. And because John did not ask whether God existed, he assumed the question in its broadest sense. In studying him, we find his basic thoughts and attitudes encompassing everything, not only so–called religious themes.

But John's God was not a vague God, he was the God of Jesus Christ, hence a God who speaks, or rather a God who has spoken in a revelation. But God's Word produces a discourse, between itself and the person who receives it. God's Word, as revealed in the Bible and the liturgy, penetrated John and took possession of him, and he in his turn spoke. God's Word necessarily goes hand in hand with the word of the believer who comments on it and receives it and is open to its meaning.

There are many aspects to John's writings and it is important, of course, to try to single them out. But in their vital core they are all the response of a man possessed by the Word. John should not therefore be seen as an exception, a freak, a way–out case. In exploring him, we are not venturing into a strange and exotic world. No, we are going to the heart of the basic question—God. But the question of God can offer the answer to another central question, 'What is man?'—at least it could do so with John.

This study will approach John along three principal lines: the first attempts to correct the commonly–held ideas regarding mysticism and mystics, the second is concerned with history, and the third with Man, with humanity.

1. There exists a false idea of mysticism, and this must be

rejected, not only through a concern for truth, but because if it were true a book like this would have to be abandoned before it was even started.

There is no need to linger over the objection that runs as follows: John of the Cross was a man of faith, so people who do not share his certainties cannot understand his thought. This assumes that faith is a certainty that, like other certainties, isolates. But if faith is a certainty, it is an absolute certainty. Hence the paradox that because faith is absolute it can answer for nothing but itself; everything, by comparison with it, seems less certain, even what is closest to it, even what someone who has the faith feels able to say about it. Faith is so strong a certainty that it shakes every other certainty and makes all descriptions of it seem inadequate. At the same time faith is critical—it operates like virulent doubt.

This being so, faith does not make a barrier between the believer and the non–believer, but rather it brings them together. This does not mean that the believer is in fact a non–believer or a pseudo–believer, nor does it mean that the believer can say to the non–believer that in fact he is a believer without knowing it (as some believers do say, with astonishing disrespect to non–believers, so as to strike a blow at atheism); no, it means that faith, despite current usage, is not something that one has or possesses. So faith is not a factor that will isolate John from future readers, but one that will draw them together.

Another objection, which is more difficult to dislodge, merits discussion at greater length—it is concerned not with faith but with the term 'mystic'. We have seen that faith is not a divisive factor (so the argument goes)—but John's experiences as a mystic, surely those are beyond our reach? Surely we should agree that only a mystic can read the works of a mystic? These remarks make hasty assumptions: first, that right deep down mysticism is an essentially paranormal experience; next, that the mystic, in his union with God, finds himself transported into the very presence of the Absolute, with no intermediary; and finally that the mystic 'knows' things that cannot be grasped by reason, and knows them in such an individual way that it is questionable whether what he has 'seen' of God can be reconciled with what theological tradition says of God.

In actual fact mysticism belongs to experience, to life as lived, and it remains to be seen in what precise circumstances. The following commonly–held propositions are false, or unacceptable without some reservations: *a* mysticism has a specific content, incommunicable in itself, but found in all forms of mysticism and all forms of religion (here we find 'reconciliation', in a false ecumenism, of the Christian, Moslem, Buddhist, etc., forms of mysticism); learned men have even cast doubt on the Christian character of John's mysticism; *b* mysticism partakes of the 'marvellous'—with miracles, ecstasies and other paranormal phenomena; *c* the mystic's goal is fusion with God, or the Absolute, so that both will become one; *d* mysticism is a way to a special sort of knowledge, more 'intuitive' but less 'certain' than rational knowledge.

If these propositions are false, then the way is clear for seeing mysticism as part of simple everyday faith. Every believer, when he says 'I believe', is taking the whole of the mystical life into his own life. Here again to forestall misunderstandings one point must be made clear—there is no intention in this book of belittling mysticism or of suggesting that God's grace is not manifested there. Rather would one say that the grace abounding in the smallest act of faith is to be seen in mysticism in a very special way.

2. The second line of approach to John puts him in his historical setting.

He was certainly not alien to the epoch in which he lived. He belonged wholly to the Church of his time and took an active part in its life, though this often brought him suffering. But there were other aspects to his life—he belonged to a religion that was itself historical, that saw itself as part of the history in which man's salvation and God's manifestation took place. There was nothing timeless about John, he was very much a Spaniard of the sixteenth century, the 'golden century' that represented the pinnacle of Spanish history. Spain, at that time, was the greatest power in the world. Charles V had been its king since 1516 and emperor of Germany since 1519. After his abdication in 1555, and until his death in 1558, he continued to exercise influence from the monastery of Yuste in Estremadura to which he withdrew when power ceased to interest him. He illustrates very well the Spain of that time—a Spain possessed of a huge empire (over which, as the saying goes, the sun never set), steeped in religious faith, at odds with the Turks and Francis I of France, and deeply disturbed by the German Lutherans. But the magnificence had something factitious about it—as it was based on gold from South America. The true productive work from the land, as initiated by the Arabs, was allowed to disappear.

The reconquest of Spain was completed in 1492. Arabic influence on the architecture and the language of the country was obviously still strong, as it was on philosophical thought owing to the commentaries on Aristotle by various Arabic scholars; but political power had come to an end. The Arabic occupation of Spain had lasted eight centuries, from 711 to 1492.

Two events dominated the sixteenth century, one important, the other relatively trivial. The important event was the Reformation and the birth of Protestantism. Martin Luther, when he died in 1546, had already been excommunicated for twenty-six years. John was then aged four. When Calvin died in 1564 John was aged twenty–two. Protestantism seems to have gained no ground in Spain due to the vigilance of the Inquisition, so it was in a world of its own that John's development took place, a world that might be called anachronistic but that did not spare him preoccupations with another quarrel the terms of which now seem remote indeed.

This trivial event was the flowering of religious movements like that of the 'enlightened' (*los Alumbrados*). These were vague and recurring tendencies rather than organised movements, and they manifested themselves in many ways—ways which no doubt represented in the religious imagination what is commonly understood by 'mysticism'. It was important for John to dissociate himself from these currents, for the battle waged by various theologians against the 'enlightened' could have given him grounds for anxiety. So he had to fight against the leanings towards 'illuminism' shown by some of the men and women under his direction. The 'illuminati' were far less important than the Reformation, yet they forced John to define very precisely his attitude to these sects. Perhaps he would not have spoken so plainly about the importance of discipline and renunciation, and about the way in which 'mystical' (in the bad sense of the word) experiences should be distrusted, if his own epoch had not been drawn towards them.

This glance at the history of the period will serve as a background. It is worth enlarging on, not for its own sake but only inasmuch as it affected John and can help us to judge how far his life, as it developed in almost a straight line, was in harmony with his thought and his writings.

What, then, of his life? Here are some of its elements:

—An extremely harsh childhood even for those hard times; the home was fatherless; he was acquainted with poverty to the point of losing a brother through starvation; another brother was sent to live with a kindly uncle who unfortunately had an appalling wife; he worked in a hospital while pursuing his studies at night. From another point of view his childhood was lived in an atmosphere of trust and love. His father and mother, Gonzalo and Catalina de Yepes, had made a marriage of love, but opposition to the match meant that they lived isolated from their families. John developed a deep intimacy with his mother and one of his brothers.

—A very rich friendship, both humanly and spiritually, with Saint Teresa of Avila; a very vital friendship, fully aware of itself and lived with extraordinary freedom, freedom with regard to each other and freedom with regard to the gossip of others. They rejoiced when circumstances brought them together and freely left each other when work demanded it. A special friendship, but not an exclusive one; Teresa's life, like John's, was marked by many attachments, and John also had a deep affection for a lay–woman, Anne of Penalosa.

—Enormous activity as founder of monasteries and reformer of the Carmelite order—an astonishingly arduous task. Reforming a religious order does not necessarily arouse charitable feelings, and early in the enterprise (1578) John had to endure imprisonment in Toledo. His thinking ripened and deepened in his cell, from which he finally escaped in fantastic circumstances with the help of a rope made from his bed–clothes. He was in captivity for nine months, a period not without significance as his spiritual growth took place during that time. He suffered further hardships from ecclesiastical administrators towards the end of his life.

- –Activity as a spiritual director where he displayed extraordinary lucidity of mind, respect for others, humour, understanding and, here too, friendship and freedom, the very salt of charity.

3. The third line of approach, the human one, can be said to be the core of this work. Studying John and learning from him should, strictly speaking, involve not only reading and interpreting his work but trying to re–live his life. Here a problem arises, for John's writings were not written for us but for sixteenth–century Spaniards, and most of all for enclosed nuns desirous of dedicating their lives to the contemplation of the God of Jesus Christ. John says explicitly at the beginning of *Ascent of Mount Carmel* that his writings were intended only for certain nuns and monks of the Carmelite order:

> Nor is my principal intent to address all, but rather certain persons of our sacred Order of Mount Carmel of the primitive observance, both friars and nuns—since they have desired me to do so.[1]

So we are outside this relationship; it is not for us to follow John's advice for it is not addressed to us, we accept what is offered—but from outside. And yet something essential can come to us without our leaving our time or place or becoming non–enclosed Carmelites! Nor is it certain that John's advice should be followed by Carmelite monks and nuns of today; neither are they the authentic recipients. So a real way must be found of interiorizing his teaching, of making it apply to us here and now. Perhaps nothing will unveil his message to those who do not want to see, but in discussing him and seeking out the core of his thought those who wish to will be able to grasp his message. It is only at this price that the desire to follow him means anything at all.

This process could be called 'making John of the Cross speak to the people of our time', which would not be wholly false but inadequate as a description of the purpose behind this book. It would involve reformulating John's thought in modern terms. But I suggest that John should be left in the past if he is truly to speak to us now. If we were to make him contemporary with us we would certainly distort him. The past is something else; the something else that is the past should not be absorbed into the present if it is to be preserved in all its distinctness. If 'making John of the Cross speak to the people of our time' means picking and choosing among

his writings the bits that are suitable for our culture, on what
principle would we make this choice? There is no satisfactory
answer.

The phrase 'speaking to our time' is unsatisfactory on several counts. It presupposes communication and non–communication between cultures without really resolving the
problems that it poses. It implies that John cannot be understood now because historically he belonged to another world.
This is rather like saying that we cannot understand the Bible
because it belongs to another era of culture—its words, even
when translated, have a different meaning for us. Yet these
texts from past cultures would (supposedly) speak to us if
they were reformulated. But—a point not sufficiently noted—
those past cultures would not in fact speak to us any more
because they would be assimilated into our own. So our
culture would simply repeat itself and re–inforce itself. Only
what is not myself can teach me anything, and above all
about myself.

So we must adopt another attitude towards John—an attitude of respect. To respect John's thought is to let it be, not
to question it, to trust it enough to believe in its good faith if
not in its truth. Respect also implies respect for one's own
and other people's independence. Respect leaves all possibilities open. Within respect we do not pretend to have an
advantage over the thought and experience of others; we
entrust them with full responsibility and do not claim to know
better than they what they believe or feel to be true.[2] To
respect someone is not to assume that he is necessarily right
or even that he is right according to his lights—this would be
to play at either domination or submission. To respect someone is to acknowledge that he knows what he is talking about.
Respect forbids me to judge. Respects bids me to leave intact
the domain reserved to the other—I shall not touch what he
says though what he says may touch me. What I do with it
is my business and what he thinks is his. His thought does
not tell me to stay in my shell, but invites me to come out so
that he can really speak to me and let me know what he
thinks, apart from all discrimination and racial or other
prejudice.

Thus respect for John's thought means refusing to try to
integrate it into our culture while admitting that it has some-

thing to say to what we are. It is not for us to pick and choose among his writings, but to accept (as best we can) everything he says as it relates to us.

Philosophy has no difficulty in paying respect. It is pre–eminently a respectful discourse. It does not appropriate to itself the realities that it deals with—it leaves them where they are, accepting their independence and retaining its own. If philosophy appropriated to itself what it examines, then the activity of philosophy would occupy a purely philosophical domain where questions and answers went round in a circle. In this case the possibility of a philosophy of the sciences (for instance) would disappear. If mathematics as explored by a philosopher ceased to be mathematics and became philosophy, then there would be no philosophy of mathematics. What is true of mathematics is true of all that philosophy treats of. If John is not true to himself when a philosopher asks questions about him, then the philosopher is wasting his time.

To summarize, or at least to assess the consequences of the philosopher's respect for John's work: the following pages are not an attempt to sit in judgement on his thought. It is not our abilities as a philosopher that will act on John's thought to rearrange it or send it back to be redrafted. Quite the reverse. It is his thought that will reach out to us to modify our philosophical ideas. Our tentative knowledge of philosophy will try to be open to John and be stirred by what he says. It is he who will come to us to transform us, he who will cause an upheaval in us, not the other way round. We must evaluate him while recognizing that what we say will not exhaust what he says any more than a lecture on a work of art can replace the work of art itself. There is no question of making points to alter anyone's idea of John. His writings will be left intact, but we shall recognize their power to alter the basic principles of philosophical study. In a sense, it is true that philosophy is concerned only with itself. But it is displaced by the object of its study. So it has to do only with itself, but insofar as it is informed and shaped by something that is not itself and that, as it were, speaks to it.

It remains to discover where and how this encounter with John will touch us, where and how we shall be roused by the words addressed to a handful of Spaniards in the sixteenth century.

We can certainly expect our ideas on man to be challenged, for John had specific ideas of his own. This is not a reference to his explicit concept of human nature which he derived partly from St Augustine and St Thomas Aquinas, both of whom he had studied at the university of Salamanca—these two probably helped more than anything to give him a convenient and standardized form of words. But what he says by means of these words is altogether different. It is a highly original idea of man that shapes his writings and will therefore shape ours.

Our implicit and rather vague knowledge concerning man, the presuppositions that we give voice to without having really thought about them, will hardly be able to stand up to John's teaching, and at the end of the day we shall surely have a deeper knowledge of what mankind is. But we are not looking for another dimension to man. Just as we do not want to rationalize John's mysticism, neither do we want to profane man's mystery. If man is mysterious he is so in his humblest state as much as in his highest powers. We cannot hope to form a correct idea of man without taking all his activities into account, and all the events that can befall him. We must listen to what John tells us, otherwise we shall miss a crucial capacity in what we call man.

As has been said, the aspect of John's work that has meant the most to us is the one concerned with man. But it probably did not mean the most to John: God, not man, was his primary concern. But if philosophy is what we say it is, then it is because the mystic is interested only in God that he can hint at an idea of man that is radically new, profound, suggestive and different.

So, to summarize, the purpose of this book is to remove a certain number of obstacles and illusions. The obstacles have to do with a notion of man based on a human reality that ignores other authentic aspects of man's nature. The illusions have to do with the nature of mysticism. Mysticism is not something 'hidden' or 'mysterious' in the sense that it is an experience that cannot be put into words. It is not the experience that defies description: it is God. Mysticism is mystical (that is to say, etymologically speaking, something

reserved for the initiated, something hidden) not because it
is itself hidden but because its object is hidden. Mysticism is
still too often confused with sentimentality and abnormal
experiences, whereas John was not so far from saying the
whole of what he had to say when he wrote:

> Love consists not in feeling great things, but in having
> great detachment and in suffering for the Beloved.[3]

In conclusion, a word of explanation about the method of
presenting John's work in this book. Each chapter is divided
into two sections—the first devoted to a theoretical account
of his thought, the second to how it worked out in practice in
his life. The first section is an attempt to distinguish between
a simple exposition of (or introduction to) John's work, and
the way in which we ourselves interpret it—or rather (to be
faithful to the principles outlined above) the way in which
this aspect of John has helped to shape our own concept of
man.

The Works of John of the Cross

John's works consist essentially of four treatises. Each is composed (1) of a poem; (2) of a commentary in which the saint
develops what he has to say. It would be difficult to decide
where his thought really lies, in the poem or in the commentary. The conclusion offered here is that his thought is to be
found neither in the poem nor in the commentary but in the
relation between the two. The commentary is not just an
elaboration of the poem but adds a meaning to it which was
not there before. Once the commentary has been read then
the poem can be re–read with the meaning unveiled in the
commentary; only then can its true meaning be discovered.

These are the four treatises:
1. *Ascent of Mount Carmel* (referred to henceforth as the
Ascent). Its commentary was probably never finished; certainly the end has never been found.
2. *Dark Night of the Soul* (referred to as the *Dark Night*).
Here the poem is the same as the poem for the *Ascent* but, as

the commentary shows, it refers to a second stage of the mystical journey. The commentary is unfinished.

3. *The Spiritual Canticle* (referred to as such). Here there is a new poem, a very beautiful one, inspired by *The Song of Songs* of the Old Testament. The commentary is complete.

4. *Living Flame of Love* (referred to as the *Living Flame*). This has its own poem, and the commentary is complete.

The four treatises follow each other and each marks an advance in the spiritual life. This could throw light on the first two commentaries being unfinished, for as soon as one stage in the mystical journey has been left behind, the following one has begun.

But the four treatises, although foundational in John's works, are supplemented by:

32 *Letters*,

10 *Poems*,

10 '*Romances*'—these, again, are poems. The *romancero* is a Spanish literary form which normally has an eight-syllable line, with the pairing lines only assonanced. The authenticity of these has been questioned.

181 *Maxims and Spiritual Sayings*, including *Points of Love*. These are brief instructions to help individual people in the community.

17 *Cautions* against the devil.

Advice to a monk that he may reach perfection, of similar inspiration as the *Cautions*.

Advice on Spirituality, not written by John himself, but guidance given by him and assembled by Fr Elisée of the province of Estramadura.

(N.B. All quotations from the works of St John of the Cross are taken from *The Complete Works of Saint John of the Cross, doctor of the Church*, edited by E. Allison Peers, in three volumes. First volume: *Ascent of Mount Carmel* and *Dark Night of the Soul*; second volume: *The Spiritual Canticle* and *Poems*; third volume: *Living Flame of Love, Cautions, Spiritual Sentences and Maxims, Letters, Sundry Documents*. Published by Burns & Oates, London, 1943. It is to these volumes that reference is made in the notes at the end of the book.)

CHAPTER ONE

I. What is Mysticism?

The word 'mysticism', as understood in this book corresponds to John's description of it in his writings. The word is used in this sense and this sense only. There is no suggestion that John was the only mystic who ever lived; this is simply a method that dispenses with the need of any further definition of mysticism.

Next, it should be remembered that John was writing as a teacher to his pupils, so he did not talk primarily about his bonds with God but about the interchange between himself and the Carmelite monks and nuns under his spiritual direction. Also, John's writings were not autobiographical; his own life did not interest him; there is nothing of the private diary in his writings, nothing in the style of, 'today I say this or that'. Yet his material is certainly based on what happened to *him*, he discusses nothing but what he himself experienced. His picture of the mystical journey, indeed, made it impossible for him to describe what he did not personally know. So we can justifiably associate the themes concerned with darkness and night with his period in prison, and if the first version of *The Spiritual Canticle*, where he speaks of deliverance, was also written in prison, then we may conclude with Georges Morel[1] that in captivity he was free with a wholly spiritual freedom.

There was no question, at least as far as the four great treatises are concerned, of John trying to enlighten anyone who had already made up his mind or who viewed himself as a special case. In everything he said John was a teacher in the noblest sense of the word. He spoke freely, giving of himself for his pupil but not addressing himself directly to him. It was for the pupil to take what he needed from the teacher's words, the teacher need not even know what was taken. So John handed over his thought to his pupil who then became master of it in his turn.

The essence of what John taught was the way to attain the highest union with God, the journey the soul[2] must undertake in order to reach God. According to John, two preliminary things should be known. The first concerns man, for 'God brings man to perfection according to the way of man's own nature',[3] so the knowledge of what human nature really is dictates the paths of the journey. The second concerns God, for people who wish to advance in the spiritual life must learn about God's ways with man. For this the *Ascent* is a 'very necessary' work, for 'herein is taught the way and purpose of God with respect to the soul'.[4] But the purpose and end of the road is more important than the road itself, for the end is God. In God there is no road—he is the absence of road, for the moment he is reached he appears as the one thing needful and the road disappears. Though God may know the predetermined paths along which man may reach him, he himself is perfect freedom, so much so that when the end is reached the journey ceases to exist:

> wherefore, upon this road, to enter upon the road is to leave the road; or, to express it better, it is to pass on to the goal and to leave one's own way, and to enter upon that which has no way, which is God. For the soul that attains to this state has no longer any ways or method, still less is it attached to such things or can be attached to them.[5]

If we understand this, then we can describe the mystical journey as being negative, analytical and critical.

To take each of these terms in turn: the mystical discourse is negative in the sense that it unfolds by saying what God is not, rather than what he is. But this can lead to confusion, for when we say what God is not, rather than what he is, are we not saying that God has no content, at least no content that can be expressed by men? Is the content of the known God empty? These questions are misleading. God had a very explicit content where John was concerned, the content enshrined in the Christian faith and proclaimed by the Church in, for instance, the Creed. What the Church describes to be

God's content, and how John's mysticism saw is, were one
and the same thing—

> faith, which alone is the proximate and proportionate
> means whereby the soul is united with God; for such is the
> likeness between itself and God that there is no other dif-
> ference, save that which exists between seeing God and
> believing in Him. For, as God is infinite, so faith sets Him
> before us as infinite; and as He is Three in One, it sets Him
> before us as Three in One.[6]

Yet, for all that, mysticism is negative, because it contrasts
believing (which derives from faith) with seeing. For mysticism, what shall ultimately be seen is the same as what is
now believed. But in relation to seeing, believing is negative.
We do not see what we believe. Hence the end of the passage
quoted above:

> and as God is darkness to our understanding, even so does
> faith likewise blind and dazzle our understanding.[7]

So the soul believes in faith what it does not see, and finds
difficulty in accepting that it sees nothing when it so ardently
wants to think that it sees something. The mystical discourse
lays down nothing except the conditions for there being
nothing to say. Yet it may seem excessive to suggest that if
the mystic has nothing to say he would do well to remain
silent. So it is necessary to show more precisely what is meant
by the process of negation.

To begin with, John had no aim of teaching anything new.
Rather, he repeated the ancient assertions of the faith. But in
repeating them he aimed at giving them fresh life, making
them new, scouring and polishing them to give them back
their brightness. But to do this he had to make us feel that
we believe the assertions of the faith though we do not see
them. There is more than one way of forgetting what we
believe. We can forget the content of our faith because we
never think about it, because it has ceased to interest us; but
there is a less obvious and more insidious type of forgetful-
ness—we can think we *know* what in fact we *believe*.[8] The
content of faith is not something we know, for to 'know' what
should be 'believed' only deadens it—fixes it and pigeonholes
it for all eternity. Far better for the content of our faith to

elude us, to be beyond our grasp, and then it will be restored to us in its truth. Man believes because he is not the source of his belief, and because faith is indestructibly linked to hope. Man must have the patience to wait before he sees, and from waiting arises faith.

If faith is hope, then man must look on faith as empty, as nothing. In fact it is himself that the believer experiences as nothing, though he does not notice his own nothingness but only the nothingness of the content of his belief, inasmuch as his belief is his, man's, own work. So what mysticism rejects is faith claiming to be a science or something known. It rejects a denial of God as revealed by faith, and it rejects a denial of God, so that God may reveal himself.

The negative aspect of mysticism is a pointer to the extremely positive aspect of the Absolute to which it aspires. The mystic's aspiration is indeterminate, because he does not know the Absolute as something he himself sets up, but as something that begets itself. God founds himself, no–one else can found him. If God is a God who reveals himself and reveals his interiority, then the act of faith is possible. At that rate mysticism is an acceptance of the God who reveals himself.

Now we see what makes for the ambiguity of mysticism— it expresses something, but what? Perhaps it can be said that mysticism brings forth what cannot be brought forth in faith. But the fact that it cannot be brought forth does not mean that there has to be silence. It remains to be shown why the believer cannot appropriate the language of faith, any more than he can simply repeat it.

Mysticism is a place; it is a place for the interchange between faith and God. To say that God is present in faith (for he has no–where else to be) is as true as to say that he is absent (because he is neither seen nor known). So mysticism lies *between* faith and God. This means that mysticism does not expect to bring forth faith, for faith is only to be found in God's Word as received in the Church. Mysticism is the measure of the distance between God and man—a distance that can be called infinite (from man's point of view) or non–existant (from God's). But it is God's elimination of the distance which gives meaning to the faith so infinitely removed from him._Through faith God makes himself present to man, immediately though invisibly. God is then The One who says who he is, and also The One who shapes man's heart so that he may be believed when he says who he is. It is taking this shaping seriously that we call mysticism. So the mystical discourse describes the human side of faith.

Thus without mysticism faith would be, not dumb, but blind—it would not see its own rootedness in man (and in God it has nothing to *see*). It is only within mysticism that faith reflects on itself, for outside mysticism it speaks only of God, never of itself.

The second characteristic of the mystical discourse is that it is analytical. In this case analysis is taken to mean making sure of one's ground, pulling on the anchor chain, deepening what one already holds. Here the believer does not advance in knowledge but digs in ever deeper at the same point. The mystical journey is made up of a series of well–charted stages, one following the other. But it is a characteristic of John's stages that they are never left behind, and it would be mistaken to suppose that the mystic abandons the stage that he has passed through. Certain texts suggest that this does happen, texts where John describes the indications showing that the time has come on to something else, to advance in a new way, because a stage has been left behind. But in fact each stage rests on and supports the previous one, unfolding itself within it while leaving intact what has been acquired.

This is what is meant by the title *Ascent*. To liken a mystic's progress to an ascent is apt, for there are two obvious features of an ascent—it goes upwards and it demands an effort against the gravity that pulls it down. But there is a third feature, less obvious but just as significant—the gradient gets steeper as it reaches the vertical. But the person who climbs vertically does not go sideways. The road that rises, and only rises, makes no advance.

This ascent on the spot, so characteristic of John's thought, is reflected in one of his most important statements. The mystic learns nothing, experiences no particular revelation, for there is no revelation but the one whose fulfilment is Jesus Christ. In an admirable passage John points out that to ask God for further revelation is to ask him to recrucify Christ—

but now, any who would enquire of Me after that manner,

and desire Me to speak to him or reveal aught to him, would in a sense be asking me for Christ again, and asking Me for more faith, and be lacking in faith, which has already been given in Christ; and therefore he would be committing a great offence against My beloved Son, for not only would he be lacking in faith, but he would be obliging Him again first of all to become incarnate and pass through life and death. Thou shalt find naught to ask of Me, or to desire of Me, whether revelations or visions; consider this well, for thou shalt find that all has been done for thee and all has been given to thee—yes, and much more also—in Him.[9]

So what is the summit of the mystical life? Surely that which is experienced between the soul and Christ and likened, in *The Spiritual Canticle*, to the Beloved and the Spouse finally reunited:

In this high estate of the Spiritual Marriage, the Spouse reveals His wondrous secrets to the soul with great readiness and frequency, and describes His works to her, for true and perfect love can keep nothing hidden.[10]

The secret revealed by the Spouse is the heart of the Christian faith, all that is best known about it, so not at all 'secret' in the ordinary sense of the word:

And thus He speaks with her and tells her how by means of the Tree of the Cross she was betrothed to Him; how He gave her herein the favour of His mercy, being pleased to die for her and making her beauteous after this manner.[11]

John does not hesitate to go further still:

For God is so desirous that the government and direction of every man should be undertaken by another man like himself, and that every man should be ruled and governed by natural reason, that He earnestly desires us not to give entire credence to the things that He communicates to us supernaturally, . . . until they pass through this human aqueduct of the mouth of man.[12]

If God taught me something personally, I would not have to believe it because God taught it, but only if the Church (other people) taught it to me in its turn.

Even more than its implicit defence of reason[13] the above quotation shows us the role entrusted by John to the human community. It is insofar as the believer belongs to a community that he can clearly express his faith. It is the community that receives God's Word in trust, and it is the community that should fully administer it, the individual having no part in this. This does not mean that there is nothing more for the individual to do—it remains for him to tread the path that is his, to open himself to what is already there in the community, to open himself to God through faith.

The work of mysticism is directed not towards deepening faith, but deepening the believer.

It is the third aspect of the mystical discourse that is critical. It is critical because it is engaged in the destruction of the make–believe. John's first task was to get rid of all false representations of God. Anything posing as God must be rejected because,

> the highest thing that can be felt and experienced concerning God is infinitely remote from God and from the pure possession of Him.[14]

The danger here is subtle but for that very reason incurs more stringent criticism. It is the danger, for instance, of a beginner being so frightened by the austerities of loss that he seeks consolation elsewhere than in loss itself. He might hope to be consoled by God, and not by loss for the sake of God. Yes, notes John, he certainly would find consolation in God, but he would find only that. His progress would be obstructed precisely by that. Nothing goes smoothly in this area, and obstructions can come from all points of the horizon. If beginners encounter aridity which, says John, is 'the pure spiritual cross',

> they flee from it as from death, and seek only sweetness and delectable communion with God. This is not self-denial and detachment of spirit, but spiritual gluttony. Herein they become spiritually enemies of the cross of Christ.[15]

A different attitude, that is to say a non–critical one, would certainly prefer God not to let the believer feast on him if this could lead him astray. But such a view would endow God with expected behaviour, a role.

The three aspects of the mystical discourse show that the believer's journey is a real one. It is not the sort of journey we would plan for ourselves, where the stages, for instance, would be forseeable. The traveller who sets out on John's journey, however active he may be, does not know where he is going. His instinct is to entrench himself in the stage he is at and fight shy of the one that lies ahead. Even if his spiritual director tells him about it, he cannot believe it is really there, for he is at *this* stage and not at another. Thus, for instance, when at a given stage the soul sees the extent of its evil, even though departing from it, it takes to hating itself and cannot believe this self–hate will ever pass. The soul prefers to doubt its director rather than believe that it is not eternally abandoned by God:

> it finds no consolation or support in any instruction nor in any spiritual master. For, although in many ways its director may show it good cause for being comforted in the blessings which are contained in these afflictions, it cannot believe him. For . . . it thinks that, as its director observes not that which it sees and feels, he is speaking in this manner because he understands it not; and so, instead of comfort, it rather receives fresh affliction.[16]

Where does this darkness come from? From the fact that the soul does not possess God, that the soul and what it is seeking never meet. What is reality if not the power that refutes our imaginings? The inexhaustibility of reality is its hallmark; of itself, it goes beyond any idea we may form of it.

According to John, the experience endured by the soul at this point is pure discrepancy, contact with pure difference. The soul's path is truly new to it. Novelty can only be based on memory: we remember what has gone before so recognize the new.[17] In this way novelty is relative novelty. So *absolute* novelty as it looms up cannot be recognized as absolute—it has to be given a place in the order of what is known. Thus the new is that which discards any system of acceptance, and the absolutely new is absolutely tasteless. That God is tasteless is proof of his complete novelty. But this absolute novelty is what has allowed the soul to make its way in safety through the dark night—

In darkness and secure.[18]

Novelty, inasmuch as it is dark, escapes the illusory. Through novelty the soul is put in touch with reality. Thus novelty shapes all experience.

There is remarkable convergence in these themes. What interests the mystic is reality and nothing but reality. Mysticism is aware of the gap between the imaginary and the real—all its active side is concentrated on the destruction of the make–believe. Mysticism is nothing but the thirst for reality in the realm of the spiritual. It aspires absolutely to reality, in other words to absolute reality. But there are presuppositions underlying its processes: it presupposes faith. In order to accept the destruction of his imaginary universe, and even in a sense of himself, the believer has to be locked to a reality which will not fade, even and especially when he cannot see it. It would be impossible to conceive of an atheistic process of this kind. There has to be a God, there has to be an Absolute. The soul is not called to a life other than its own. The soul truly lives, conformably with what it is, but in God. Which is why no–one should abandon, however slightly, his own nature and the use of his reason:

> Wherefore on the day of Judgement God will punish for their many faults and sins many souls with whom He may quite habitually have held converse here below, and to whom He may have given much light and virtue; for, as to those things that they have known that they ought to do, they have been neglectful, and have relied upon that converse that they have had with God and upon the virtue that He has given them.[19]

II. John as Spiritual Director

John had two main activities—spiritual guidance and, closely associated with it, the reform of the Carmelite order initiated by Teresa of Avila. Teresa enlisted John's co–operation to carry out among the monks the reform she herself had undertaken with the nuns.

The Carmelites were a mendicant order like the order of Preachers, the Augustinians and the Franciscans, also founded in the twelfth century. Like the other three, their basic rule was to rely on the generosity of the Christian community for their support. Added to this was an intense contemplative life. But ever since their foundation in Palestine (whence their name, after Mount Carmel[1]) much relaxation of the original rule had found its way into the order. A similar development had taken place among the Carmelite nuns founded in 1451. So the work initiated by Teresa and John took the form of a return to the sources. The reformed Carmelites, called the 'discalced'—to distinguish them from the unreformed ones who wore sandals (the 'calced')—founded many monasteries, a venture not achieved without collisions, sometimes violent.

Though the reform was John's primary work, it was inseparable from his work as spiritual director, in that one was the product of the other. It was necessary to counsel monks and nuns to achieve reform, and it was necessary to achieve reform so as to counsel monks and nuns in accordance with the spirit of the order.

In the treatises that form the body of his doctrine, John gives his views about spiritual directors—those who direct novices as novice–masters and monks and nuns as confessors. They are necessary, as mysticism is a road that no–one can embark on alone, and in this field God wants people to help each other.[2] But spiritual directors are often unaware of how they beget disciples who mysteriously resemble them, notes John.[3] Here we are dealing with spiritual fatherhood, but the son becomes a father in his turn.[4] The director gives the disciple much more than he supposes, thus the disciple escapes from the director because the director escapes from himself.

This is not all. The spiritual director has his own idea of God, but no–one has a correct idea of God, for God goes beyond any conceivable framework. As John notes,[5] it is easy to wait for God where he is not, to believe he should behave thus and not otherwise, when in fact God is freedom itself and wholly unpredictable. Here again the disciple escapes from his director because God himself escapes from him. The director risks imposing an idea of God on his disciple, whereas there is no idea of God. Nothing can be said about a person's being, especially when that person is God. God cannot be measured, but we can be measured by God.[6]

So, however close to his disciple a director may be, he is infinitely distant from him. Sometimes he can do nothing for him. He wants to help him but can do nothing during those times when the disciple is plunged into the dark night where he experiences total abandonment by God. Then all the consoling things that a director can say turn back against him.[7]

Spiritual directors are no more than men. When they find themselves out of step with their penitents, either behind them or ahead of them, they may have no idea what is going on inside them. The point is that the mystic and his director are not two, but three. The Holy Spirit overshadows them. So for the director, the other is to be respected not only as a human being but because all the otherness of God is within him.

Despite these difficulties, or because of them, John was an outstanding director all his life and in many different places. From the beginning, when he was first enlisted by Teresa, he filled the office of confessor and director. He counselled the nuns at Teresa's newly–opened convent at Duruelo (1567) when he was only twenty–five years old.

In mid–October, 1570, Teresa founded the convent at Pastrana, the first large novice–house of the reform. At the same time the convent of Alba de Tormes was being prepared for its inauguration on 25 January 1571. There, too, John was the nuns' spiritual director. But soon he had to take up a new post as rector of the college of Alcala, founded on 1 November 1570. He went there in April, before the official opening. After a while he had to return to Pastrana where the novices were in revolt against the excessive penances imposed by their novice–master. After re–establishing spiritual peace, John went away again.

On 6 October 1571 Teresa was preparing to enter the convent of the Incarnation at Avila where there were 130 'hungry and frightened' nuns. They were frightened of Teresa, whom the apostolic delegate responsible for the appointment had sent them—they were frightened of finding themselves subjected to the harsh rule of the 'discalced' Carmelites. However Teresa fell ill and appealed to John to help her with the nuns, and soon his soothing presence made itself felt. He wrote instructive notes for the nuns, alas now lost. And he lived with a companion in a little house beside the convent.

This was the period when tension with the 'calced' Carmelites became acute. In a spirit of conciliation, John proposed to resign as confessor at the Incarnation—an extremely coveted post. But the most crucial twist of the quarrel resulted in his arrest. His imprisonment interrupted for several months his activity as director and confessor. This was resumed in mid–October 1578 when he went to Andalusia to take up new responsibilities. He stopped at Beas, staying with some nuns. Finally he reached Calvario (Jaen), the monastery entrusted to his care. As soon as he arrived he moderated the rigours of the penitential exercises and devoted himself to the development of a spirit of love and trust in the community.

In addition to his work as prior at Calvario, every Saturday he visited the nuns at Beas. Their testimony concerning his guidance is unanimous—they were delighted with him. For each of them he drew Mount Carmel as an allegorical diagram of the mystical ascent, in the manner of 'maps of the tender passion'. In 1579 he went to Baeza at the request of the university. A convent–cum–college had recently been founded there which was soon to be transformed into a hospital, due to an epidemic of the plague. Nursing the sick became one of John's most cherished occupations.

So he left Calvario but remained spiritual director of the nuns at Beas, at their urgent request. As the travelling distance was now much greater, he went there when his work permitted rather than every Saturday, but was able to stay for longer periods at a time. Another monk always went with him and on the way they sang hymns or psalms or verses composed by John. For the nuns he wrote brief notes of spiritual guidance, and at this time he was also writing the *Cautions*. On the way from Baeza to Beas they stopped by at Calvario so that John could keep in touch with those he had directed. At Teresa's request he also visited the nuns at Caravaca, in the province of Murcia, and heard their confessions. And he told them the story of his imprisonment. Then he was elected prior at Granada where he was wholly successful with the novices who bore witness to his affection for them.

Between 1585 and 1588 his activities increased.

He went to Lisbon to attend a chapter of the order. Returning home to Granada he made a detour via Malaga so that he could console the nuns who had been greatly upset by a suicide among their number—Catalina Evangelista. As the whole of Andalusia had been put in his charge, he made a point of visiting all the convents. Everywhere he enforced the new provincial's directive, to be summed up in one word—rigour. But soon he had to go to Madrid for a chapter. He fell ill before his departure, went all the same, and returned to Andalusia to die in 1591.

So a contemplative's life, as seen from the outside, does not at all fit in with what the word 'mystic' might suggest if understood in terms of hermit–like solitude. John was an extremely active man, warm–hearted and spreading good–will all around him. And on his travels, so it is said, he changed the lives of prostitutes and intervened to stop fights. As to his teaching throughout this busy life as a spiritual director, we know what it was—the mystical journey. We know it through the contemporary accounts of monks and nuns as well as through his own writings. His writings formed such an intimate part of his teaching that, far from concealing a work in progress, he would put it at the disposal of any convent where he was. This is not the place to summarize his teaching as it appears in the treatises, but rather to try to show how it was received and the main lines it followed as he counselled his penitents in oral talks and written notes.

Its development can be traced in various areas of guidance, starting with what could be called his defence of emptiness, of frustration, of aridity:

> More does God esteem in thee an inclination towards aridity and suffering for love of Him than all the consolations and spiritual visions and meditations that may be thine.[8] Renounce thy desires and thou shalt find that which thy heart desires. How knowest thou if thy desire is according to God?[9]

So we must withdraw from everything, expect nothing from our feelings, 'but let Christ Crucified be sufficient for thee'.[10] Let there be nothing but silence and aridity in the disciple. Thus there is a whole strand in John's thought that is extremely rigorous, a whole strand in his spirituality that belongs to the desert and the night. There is nothing to expect but the night, the desert, privation and suffering. God is himself a principle of frustration.

But there is something beyond frustration; there are texts that speak of great plenitude. Here is one of them, overflowing with joy, freedom and abundance:

> With what procrastinations dost thou wait, since thou canst of a certainty love God in thy heart? . . . Mine are the heavens and mine is the earth; mine are the people, the righteous are mine and mine are the sinners; the angels are mine and the Mother of God, and all things are mine; and God Himself is mine and for me, for Christ is mine and all for me. What, then, dost thou ask for and seek, my soul? Thine is all this, and it is all for thee. Despise not thyself nor give thou heed to the crumbs which fall from thy Father's table. Go thou forth and do thou glory in thy glory. Hide thee therein and rejoice and thou shalt have the desires of thy heart.[11]

Various comments are required. First, that this passage says the exact opposite of the previous one. In fact they should be taken together. People who listen only to one miss the whole point. To them is addressed the following thundering statement:

> He that seeks not the cross of Christ seeks not the glory of Christ.[12]

Though taken together, these two aspects should be seen chronologically. The words about aridity should come before the words about plenitude, which can only be said *then*. This is probably why John says much more about aridity than plenitude, for there are many more people who quail at entering the dark night than come out on the other side, and those who do come out on the other side have less need of advice than the others. Moreover there is another reason for the sharp contrast between the two words. John was writing for specific people who needed specific counsel and exhortation to set them free, and the more incisive his words, the more they helped his pupils to search themselves and discover where the application lay. But though John's writings were intended for specific people, there is nothing secret or confidential about them, for they were also intended for all. And though the two words, aridity and plenitude, are in contrast, they tell of the same love of God.

They are not John's only pair of opposites; there is also obedience/freedom. In his *Cautions* John's definition of obedience is extremely severe and might seem to show a narrowness of spirit that makes us tremble:

> Let the second caution [against the devil] be that thou never consider thy superior as less than if he were God, be the superior who he may, for to thee he stands in the place of God.[13]

But here comes the antidote: a convent would be dead indeed if no–one raised his voice in criticism:

> Spiritual Sayings, no. 12: . . . And he said he was afraid that to train religious in this way was a mark of the devil, for if they are trained by this method of fear, their superiors dare not warn or reprove them when they go astray . . .
> Spiritual Sayings, no. 13: So true is this, that the good father, Fray John of the Cross, would say that he would prefer that such friars should not profess in the Order [which would become completely relaxed and ruined] . . . And this (he would say) is clearly seen when nobody raises protests in chapter, but everything is ceded and allowed to pass.[14]

True freedom can only develop within, not against, obedience just as true obedience can only exist as a function of freedom.

A third pair of 'opposites' can be found in the context of the community, which is seen as both very important and very dangerous. A community must be wholly possessed by God's transcendence, not an end in itself but a means for serving God. Yet paradoxically it is only when a community is a means that it can also be an end and love of neighbour can come into its own. On the other hand love of God must be all–important even if it disrupts the community as such and keeps the monks or nuns apart from each other. Whence the texts where the community as such is repudiated:

> Love to be unknown both by thyself and by others. Never look at the good or at the evil of others.[15]

Great wisdom is it to be able to keep silence and to look
neither at the words nor at the deeds nor at the lives of
others.[16]
Live in this world as though there were in it but God and
thy soul, so that thy heart may be detained by naught that
is human.[17]

And again:

> . . . he must needs live in the monastery as if no other
> person lived there; and thus he should never intermeddle,
> either in word or in thought, with the things that happen
> in the community, nor with those of individuals, nor must
> he take note of anything concerning them, be it good or
> evil, nor of their personal qualities.[18]

Only God must be loved. And even this exclusive love for
God contains a 'contradiction'—

All for Me and naught for thee.[19]
All for Thee and naught for me.[20]

We could take this as meaning, all the suffering for me, no
suffering for Christ, all the glory for Christ, no glory for me.
But it would surely be presumptuous to want to take Christ's
place in his passion. A better interpretation might be, all the
glory is for thee, no glory is for me, and because of that, all
that thou hast suffered is for me, and thou hast kept nothing
for thyself. As soon as we settle for one interpretation we are
drawn back to the other.

But to return to John's attitude to the community. The
believer's isolation with God does not imply indifference to
other people; on the contrary, it implies true charity and true
love, so true is it that the relationship with others should be
independent and free. So we find passages in John extolling
the community and love for others if only to echo John the
Evangelist: 'He that loves not his neighbour, abhors God'.[21]
And here is another passage:

> And such is the fervour and power of the love of God that
> those of whom He takes possession can never again be
> limited by their own souls or contented with them. Rather
> it seems to them a small thing to go to Heaven alone;
> wherefore they strive with yearnings and celestial affections

and the keenest diligence to bring many to Heaven with them.[22]

We find the same alternation between extremes in John's own life. He was capable of great severity. From Duruelo onwards he carried out his responsibilities with firmness and authority. He counselled, but he also corrected and punished. Yet he had a lot of common–sense regarding punishment and reprimand. He recommended his pupils not to flee from their faults or the consequences of these but to face them squarely without fear or anguish.[23] And in another convent it is reported that he was quick to punish and would not tolerate any breaking of the rule.

As against all this we have accounts of his gentleness. He was affectionate with the monks and attentive to his neighbour. When the plague broke out at Baeza in 1580 eighteen monks were confined to their beds. He obtained meat for them, prepared it, and also amused them with funny stories. If one of them had no appetite, John gave him a list of everything on the menu until something took his fancy. He nursed Brother Gerardo day and night. He consoled his monks and promised one of them that the members of his family stricken by the plague would not die—a promise that came true (but, as if in a kind of exchange, John's mother died).

An even more significant trait: as he never excused forbidden chatter, yet disliked having to punish, he rattled his rosary or even coughed when approaching monks who were talking during silent periods so that they would not be caught. When he punished it was with sorrow, and hoping that others would intervene in favour of the defaulter. It was generally believed that he acted in this way not out of weakness but with definite purpose.

He often went walking with the monks in the country, telling them that if he kept them too enclosed they would want to leave. In any case he loved the country and loved nature, and got some woodland and pools allotted to him where he could walk and meditate. He often took a brother with him and teased him affectionately if he became tired or sleepy or bored. He granted the monks whole days of recreation when they could picnic out of hours—though he himself abstained, he was happy for them. He also enjoyed celebrating feast–days, especially Christmas.

He was the first to do the humble jobs, the washing–up, the housework, cleaning out the lavatories. He took pleasure in paving the floors of the cells and worked as a mason with his brother in building an aqueduct that still stands in Granada. But whatever penury might result for the convent, he always interrupted lucrative work of this kind as soon as he was needed by the monks—for they were considerably more important buildings than those made of stone. The monks therefore loved him and always welcomed him with joy (save for the few exceptions which will be discussed later). He was deeply concerned with both the spiritual and material welfare of those he directed. A sign of affection—at the end of his life the nuns shared among themselves what he left on his plate.

We can now form some sort of picture of John's spiritual direction, a picture governed by contrasts, but these contrasts are only disconcerting if they leave a void, a blank. The void can be filled by two freedoms that meant a great deal to John—God's freedom which must not be thwarted in its unfathomable designs on the individual, and the individual's freedom which must be left to him, with no–one wishing to live or speak in his place. John, as a spiritual director, was inspired by a twofold respect—respect for God and respect for the person.

CHAPTER TWO

I. God's Absence is still God

The *Ascent* and the *Dark Night* show the mystical journey at its most rigorous; small wonder that the legend grew up of a John driven by dark and stormy emotions. Nor is there any point in minimizing the severity of the first phase of the journey. Yet its meaning is a far cry from the romantic interpretation suggested by the legend: it may be shrouded in night but it is at the opposite pole from despair.

At first the soul feels itself being devoured by a beast and having nothing to do with the God of Love. Divine action

> destroys and consumes its [the soul's] spiritual substance, and absorbs it in deep and profound darkness. As a result of this, the soul feels itself to be perishing and melting away, in the presence and sight of its miseries, by a cruel spiritual death, even as if it had been swallowed by a beast and felt itself being devoured in the darkness of its belly.[1]

But once past this crisis the soul discovers itself again. By the end of the journey the believer is drawing very near to happiness, in the strongest and simplest sense of the word,

> for the soul in this state sees that these things [the gifts of God] are in some measure like the white stone which S. John [the Evangelist] says will be given to him that conquers, and on the stone a name shall be written, which no man knoweth saving he that receiveth it. This alone can be said thereof with truth, that it savours of eternal life.[2]

This is a quotation from the *Apocalypse*,[3]

To him who conquers I will give . . . a white stone, with a

new name written on the stone which no one knows except him who receives it.

A rich and suggestive text, very much in John's style, where the name on the stone is the name of the soul, the name by which God calls it to intimacy with himself. So it is its whole individuality, its whole egocentric individuality (if one may so put it) that is restored to the soul, and in amazing circumstances.

This impression is strengthened in the *Living Flame* where God becomes the soul's servant:

> it now feels God to be so solicitous in granting it favours, and addressing it in such precious and delicate and endearing words, and magnifying it with favour upon favour, that it believes that He has no other soul in the world to favour thus, nor aught else wherewith to occupy Himself, but that He is wholly for itself alone.[4]

In the course of its journey, and right up to the end, the soul has been beset with every illusion it could dream up. But here, in the *Living Flame*, there is no illusion—the illusion is what is really happening. So much so that one sometimes feels that the effacing of the believer before God has given way to the effacing of God before the believer:

> He loves thee with the greatest humility, and with the greatest esteem, making thee His equal, joyfully revealing Himself to thee, in these ways, which are His knowledge, by means of this His countenance full of graces, and saying to thee, in this His union, not without great rejoicing on thy part: I am thine and for thee, and I delight to be such as I am that I may be thine to give Myself to thee.[5]

In this passage we have reached one of the essential points of faith—one that goes beyond the previously–formed ideas of God. Here it is not a question of loving God–in–the–highest, God the almighty and remote Being. The great marvel here is not loving the higher–than–oneself, not loving God, but being loved by him. Here we have a fantastic reversal whereby the greater loves the lesser, and loves him with humility, esteem and joy—a reversal unthinkable to an ancient Greek, for instance, for in Aristotle's view friendship was possible only from the lesser to the greater, or between equals. Who could have conceived of such a thing! God is *humble,* and from his humility before men he draws his glory and his joy in being God.

These words are so outrageously daring that they demand very careful study. It would not be at all right to confront John, the alledgedly doleful exponent of the dark night, with another John finally appropriating God for his own glory. This would be a demoniacal idea and, pushed to its extreme, would encourage us to think—before we had really studied them—that John's writings are not so straightforward as they seem. However, unguarded assertions concerning the glory of the believer who has arrived at the pinnacle of his ascetic journey would overlook the asceticism itself, it would overlook the fact that no moment of the journey can fade, that the mystical discourse is analytical, and that the believer's eclipse in the early part of the journey is still maintained at the heart of his glory. The condition that makes it possible to propound the believer's supremacy is *first* to have established God's supremacy. In other words, although it is true to say that the primary object of John's writings is the believer, it is no less true to say that it is God.

To eliminate this apparent contradiction the notion of the *gift* must be introduced. The gift made by God to the soul is not an ordinary one—it is the gift of himself. God gives himself to the believer so wholly and with so little regret that the believer (so God implies) can do what he likes with him; he gives himself to the believer so unstintingly that the believer, in his turn, can give him to whomever he chooses:

> for in this state the soul sees that God truly belongs to it, and that it possesses Him with hereditary possession, with rightful ownership, as an adopted Child of God, through the grace that God gave to it, and it sees that, since He belongs to it, it may give and communicate Him to whomsoever it desires of its own will.[6]

But if the soul is able thus to perceive the gift that has been given it, this is because it loves God more than it loves itself. Free to give God to whomsoever it will, the soul offers him to the one it loves, to God himself, and thus it gives Him to its Beloved, who is the very God that gave Himself to it.[7]

By making this gift to God, the soul enhances the gift God makes to it. Indeed the soul lives by giving God to God and so receives in addition the power to offer God to God. It lives by being able to give God a gift that is not derisory (as any gift would be that it itself could give), a gift truly commensurate with God, God himself—and nothing is more satisfying to the soul. But the soul receives still more—the knowledge that God rejoices in it and is nourished by it, since he receives himself from it. This is a more startling gift than at first it seemed, for the activity of giving God to God is not something that happens between God and the soul as if from outside. Giving God to God is the very activity of God, it partakes of God's inward being, of the Trinity, Father, Son and Holy Spirit,

> [the soul] may breathe in God the same breath of love that the Father breathes in the Son and the Son in the Father, which is the same Holy Spirit. . . . The soul united and transformed in God breathes in God into God the same Divine breath that God, when she* is transformed in Him, breathes into her in Himself.[8]

So the soul lives like the Trinity. But the Trinity *is* this relational life. Hence the soul is the Trinity. And here we have the solution, or the partial solution, to that question, for if the soul becomes the Trinity it is not surprising that God and the believer can be celebrated together. God and the believer can *both* be the object of John's writings—we do not have to choose between them or risk contradicting ourselves. So the mystical discourse is a single discourse with God and the believer, since they form but one. The believer's presence

---

* *Translator's note*: The soul is given the pronoun 'it' by the translator of this book—a choice that had to be made as the French 'elle' can be rendered either by 'it' or 'she'. Allison Peers, on the other hand, in his translation of John of the Cross's works, and presented with the same choice from the Spanish 'ella', usually, though not always, favoured 'she', which is more in tune with the poetic quality of the saint's writing.

is as vital to the development of mysticism as God's presence, for the presence is the same.

But we must beware, for the assertion that God and the believer are the single object of the mystical discourse solves only half the problem. We can see how God and the believer make one, but it still has to be proved that John's idea is not diabolical! True, showing that the believer does not claim to supplant God or put God at his service provides a partial answer—giving God to God does not suppose domination over God. Yet the ambiguity remains.

But if God and the believer are celebrated equally in one same process and one single intuition—if God and the believer are celebrated simultaneously and following the same mode of being—then the believer's divinization is God's divinization, and John would seem to be making common cause with pantheism—every believer is God, God is every believer. This is a grave problem, and a distinction must be maintained between the believer and God.

But here again we have a seeming contradiction which could be stated this way: how is it possible to think these two assertions simultaneously, (1) the believer and God are one; (2) the believer and God are and remain essentially distinct? If the believer is divinized by the gift of God, how can he not be a god? Unless we answer this question, mysticism would be reduced to one of these alternatives: either God would fade away and be eaten up by men, or man would fade into a divinity not very different from himself. In either case mysticism would have demiurgic overtones. And nothing could be more foreign to John's thought, which, after all, claimed to be absolutely Christian!

John was aware of this problem and from the beginning of the *Ascent* laid the basis of an answer—namely, that although they are the same, God and the believer retain essentially different modes of being,

> so that pure transformation [of the soul in God] can be wrought . . . through participation of union, albeit not essentially.[9]

In order that both these things may be better understood, John makes a comparison:

A ray of sunlight is striking a window . . . If it [the window] be wholly pure and clean, the ray of sunlight will transform it and illumine it in such wise that it will itself seem to be a ray and will give the same light as the ray. Although in reality the window has a nature distinct from that of the ray itself, however much it may resemble it, yet we may say that that window is a ray of the sun or is light by participation.[10]

Just as the window is luminous with the light that strikes it, so that it becomes indistinguishable from the light, though without ceasing to be a window, in the same way man divinized by God remains a man—and is only God by participation.

Thus we must decide what participation in the life of the Trinity means, so that the two assertions—on the identity and the difference between the believer and God—can both be valid. And to do this we must return to what John said about the glorification of the believer, and look more closely at what he meant by the believer's transformation in God.

The first point to be noted is the extraordinary intimacy achieved by God in the gift of himself. John compares this intimacy not to a presence (for there has to be a certain distance between what is present and what it is present to) but to a flood. The believer's being is invaded by God as water invades everything before it. The flood is the flood of God's voice. The choice of language here is suggestive for, by contrast with what I *see*, what I *hear* reaches the inmost part of me, it reaches my very core. What is said to me I understand with my inmost being, with the very heart of me. So man is assailed and flooded by God's voice as by a river or torrent,

> it must be known that she [the soul] feels herself to be assailed by the torrent of the Spirit of God in this case, in such a manner, and taken possession of thereby with such force, that it seems to her that all the rivers of the world are coming upon her and assailing her, and she feels that all her actions are whelmed thereby, and all the passions which she had aforetime.[11]

But for that very reason God remains God. He holds himself infinitely remote from the soul. By giving himself, he disappears. His being remains distinct, says John in the *Ascent*, and of this it is possible to have a clearer idea, and one easier to chart in the themes now before us. God gives himself and withholds himself at the same time—God truly gives himself and yet remains out of reach. The object of the believer's yearning is hidden by no more than a 'thin web'. The soul cries:

> Perfect me now if it be thy will
> Break the web of this sweet encounter.[12]

But the web will not break. In any case, what would breaking it achieve? Nothing but the believer's death. But it is not actual death that responds to the invitation to death—it is faith. The hope to see God will be answered only later. In the gift that is given him here below, God again escapes from the soul and hides himself so deeply within it that the believer cannot savour God closely but just feels him gently moving within him,

> God dwells secretly in all souls and is hidden in their substance; for, were this not so, they would be unable to exist.[13]

So the believer carries God within him, moving gently like a baby in its mother's womb. But the baby's birth would be the believer's death, so God remains absolutely hidden, without showing himself. How does he manage to hide so well? John's answer is brilliant and highly paradoxical, but also very powerful: God is so well hidden in the soul *because he is not there*. Where the paradox reaches its peak is when John adds that it is inasmuch as God is not in the believer that he is in him.

Yet again, in solving one contradiction we seem to have fallen into another. Yet again we must look closely at God's gift of himself to the believer, though here we reach the topmost peak higher than which we cannot climb.

What happens to the believer when God gives himself to him? At first the believer seems able to contain God—man, after all, has the tools for receiving God, his understanding, his memory and his will, the three basic elements, according to St Augustine. For John these three elements had enormous meaning—he likens the memory, the understanding and the will to hollow caverns. But man was unaware of all this. Before God showed himself to him, man was unaware that he could receive him. His emptiness had never been put to the test in the course of his ordinary life, not in any way at all. It was God who had to tell him about his depths as a man, who had to show him the emptiness within him. Then and only then the space for God could open—inasmuch as it had not already been filled:

> With respect to the *first cavern* which we here describe—namely, the understanding—its emptiness is thirst for God, and, when the understanding is made ready for God, this is so great that David[14] compares it to that of the hart, finding no greater thirst wherewith to compare it, for the thirst of the hart is said to be most vehement.[15]
> The *second cavern* is the will, and the emptiness thereof is hunger for God, so great that it causes the soul to swoon.[16]
> The *third cavern* is the memory, whereof the emptiness is the melting away and languishing of the soul for the possession of God.[17]
> The capacity, then, of these caverns is deep; for that which they are capable of containing, which is God, is deep and infinite; and thus in a certain sense their capacity will be infinite, and likewise their thirst will be infinite, and their hunger also will be infinite and deep, and their languishing and pain are an infinite death.[18]

These infinite caverns, infinitely empty since they are capable of containing God, will never be filled in this life. Everything is given, but it would be equally true to say that nothing is given. Even having reached the *Living Flame* the soul

> lives in hope, and thus cannot fail to be conscious of something that is lacking, it sighs deeply, though with sweetness and joy, in proportion as it still lacks complete possession of the adoption of the sons of God.[19]

More precisely, the filling of these caverns is their opening. We cannot receive God but he can open in us the infinity of the space he needs. Better—since without God this infinite space would not be opened—this is his way of approaching us, his way of moving into us. So the opening of the emptiness has two characteristics, (1) the emptiness is irredeemably empty, there is nothing in it; (2) it is empty of God and only of him. So it speaks only of God and in a way that is commensurate with him. Thus the emptiness of God is a yearning for him.

So we have reached the end. The horrible groaning emptiness, the infinite death, is the emptiness, the absence of God in man, and therefore the means by which man is in touch with God. God's absence is his presence. Through his immense yearning for God, man already possesses God. Hence John's question, if the soul already possesses God, why should it yearn for him?[20] It is because God's presence exists through his absence. God's extreme remoteness creates his intimacy at the heart of man. The infinitely remote opens man to the essentially close, without in any way diminishing the distinction between the two, but rather emphasizing it. The mystic knows better than the rest of us how far are God's thoughts from ours.[21] Anything that yearns for what is absent fulfils itself in what is not there, yet without making this present in any sense that would alter the immensity of the distance.

The glorification of the believer is achieved at a distance from God, so it does not modify God's transcendence however intimately God is contained within the believer. The believer can disappear in God only in the same way, that is apart from his own destruction, at a distance from his own death. Thus can we understand the following passage in the *Dark Night*:

> for communications which are indeed of God have this property, that they humble the soul and at the same time exalt it.[22]

So another factor must be brought into the relationship between God and the believer, one that will avoid the stumbling-block caused by the assertion that God is in the believer inasmuch as he is not in the believer. God's absence can be seen as a crucial part of the relationship.

It goes without saying that God's absence cannot be an object of the mystical discourse—this would be tantamount to saying that mysticism is a form of atheism. God's absence only means anything if it is God's absence for the believer. Three factors are required: God, God's absence, and the believer. Taken two by two they are contradictory, but as soon as the third is introduced it acts as mediator and gives the other two a basis for survival.

1. God/God's absence. It is contradictory to wish for a discourse concerned with God if God is absent and out of reach. But this is solved if the discourse includes a believer possessed by a God who does not show himself. The discourse will have a content while being faithful to God's absence. God can be both present and absent if there is anyone for whom he is absent, and we are not just playing with words when we say that God is present in himself but absent for man. This absence is crucial for, as things stand, it is the only context in which God can appear. God's absence is the way he is present to man. The discourse can thus be wholly centred on God and God's absence once the believer is in the middle of the picture.

2. God/believer. It is impossible to hold a discourse directed wholly to God and wholly to the believer as if they were but one single object. Here it is God's absence that saves the situation. To look at God's absence is the same as to look at God. Yet the person for whom the absence exists will disclose himself at the same time and the text will speak of the believer painfully empty of God.

3. Believer/absence. Finally, if a man's belief is empty he is holding discourse with an illusion, unless the third factor, God, is postulated as the principle that obliges faith to believe and speak.

All this is not as strange as it seems, for in fact we know well the complex relationship existing between one person and the absence of another. We live all the time with the presence deep within us of people who are not us, who never will be us, although all our activity reaches out to them. This relationship is called desire. In fact we could summarize everything we have said in one sentence: the soul, as John sees it, is defined by its capacity to desire God. Obviously it remains for us to say what we mean by desire, and in what sense God can be called desirable, for this word covers a multitude of meanings.

We could do worse than to ponder, with John of the Cross, this well-known and traditional proposition (though slightly reworded): God gives himself to us truly, but without ever

changing faith into knowledge, or hope into fulfilment. Faith
will pass away, hope will pass away, but charity (which is
glorified desire and the very truth of desire) shall never pass
away.

II. John of the Cross and God's Absence

Nothing grows except through the death and resurrection of
what we are. We must continually die and rise again, leave
everything yet lose nothing, gain everything by losing everything. Even in the simplest psychological life we advance only
be means of crises—often we emerge from them victorious,
but sometimes we remain imprisoned, bogged down, incap-
able of coming out on the other side. In the view of faith, this
is the work within us and around us of the Master of the
world and of history—work accomplished by God's silence.
In real life God's silence is his absence and the seeming
absence of meaning in the events we experience.

God's absence is a commonplace in our lives, not some
terrible and exceptional calamity but the normal texture of
our being. In a sense God's absence is the withdrawal of his
grace, but there is no withdrawal of grace which is not still
a grace, since it is in death and through death that we rise
again. But what is death if not God's withdrawal from us, if
it be true that death is the wages of sin, the wages of abandonment by God? So there is a very special manifestation of
God's absence—death, and its foretaste, suffering. So to question oneself about God's absence which in John's life was his
presence, is to question oneself about suffering.

It is important to realize that darkness and pain and failure
were not by any means passing phases in John's life. The
journey he described was certainly wholly completed by him,
but his life bears witness to the fact that the dark night was
with him from start to finish. His union with God brought no
relief from tribulation though it can certainly be said that his
dark night had its brightness, and that at the very heart of
suffering he encountered the fullness of light. This confirms
what emerged in the theoretical part of this analysis—that
God's absence never ceases, the mystical dark night is never
interrupted. The stages are not necessarily arranged chrono-

logically—each remains very much alive at each point of the journey. There is a sense in which the mystical life moves vertically. God is encountered at the very heart of the night, there is no stepping aside from pain and suffering except into itself. John found his contact with God in God's absence. There are no economies where suffering is concerned. There is no getting round suffering while God is beyond our reach.

John's father, Gonzalo de Yepes, was a nobleman. He was a regular visitor to the market at Medina del Campo and always stayed with a widow at Fontiveros, a large village of 5,000 inhabitants. She lived by her weaving and looked after a young orphan girl, Catalina Alvarez. Gonzalo married Catalina in spite of the social difference and family opposition. After the marriage his family r·fused to see him so the young couple remained in the widow's house and lived with her until she died. In 1530 they had a son, Francisco, and some time between 1531 and 1541 they had a second son, Luis. In 1542 John was born. By then the family was poorer than ever.

Before long Gonzalo fell ill and died. Catalina Alvarez de Yepes was left alone with her three children and without any means of support. The eldest was then about thirteen. So the future John of the Cross would hardly have known his father, being aged about one when he died.

Utterly without resources, Catalina decided to seek help outside Fontiveros. She turned to two of her husband's brothers, one a priest living in Torrijos in the region of Toledo, the other a doctor living in Galvez. The priest showed Catalina the door, so she travelled the fifteen miles to Galvez where she was received with affection. As the doctor had no children of his own, nor even more distant descendants, he promised to take in and care for the eldest of his nephews and assure him some kind of future. Catalina stayed for a while before returning to Fontiveros with her two youngest.

After a year back she went to Galvez having received no news of her son. Once alone with his mother, Francisco told her how unhappy he was with his uncle and how detested he was by his aunt. Catalina took him home and the whole family was together again at Fontiveros. The three children went to school but Francisco did not do well and his mother removed him. Luis died, probably of hunger. Catalina left Fontiveros for good and set up home at Arevalo where she and Francisco found work in weaving. Francisco was now twenty, and restless, but underwent a sudden conversion. Hunger was always at the door. The economic difficulties became so bad that they had to leave Arevalo and find some other means of support. John was now aged eight.

After leaving Arevalo, the three of them arrived at Medina del Campo, a town of 30,000 inhabitants. This was the lively commercial city visited by Gonzalo, a market centre for the whole of Spain and even for Europe, in particular the Netherlands (which were Spanish) but also France, Italy and Portugal. All three of them wove, but the silken head–dresses that they created were not enough to feed them.

At Medina there was a School of Doctrine, similar to the ones in Salamanca, Valladolid, Palencia and Guadalajara. These were boarding schools for poor children, usually orphans, where they were fed, clothed, lodged and taught 'Christian doctrine'—hence their name. It was there that John began his education, and he continued it at Salamanca as a novice with the Carmelites where he was to be ordained priest.

When John began his career, it had been as a spiritual director and reformer of the Carmelite order.

To begin with, the 'calced' helped the 'discalced' Carmelites, but later this help was to become less defined. From this halcyon period date the foundations authorized by the General of the order, Juan Bautista Rubeo—Duruelo, Mancera, Pastrana, Alcala, Altamira, la Roda, Almodóvar del Campo. All this was achieved without difficulty, but major tensions soon began to show themselves. At first the causes seemed trivial enough. It was not any fundamental problems that caused the trouble or, if so, they were soon envenomed by personal questions, matters of prestige, blunders on the part of the better–intentioned.

This is what happened.

Two Dominicans had been appointed by the Pope as apostolic visitors, Pedro Fernandez for Castile and Francisco de Sargas for Andalusia; their brief was to visit the 'calced' and 'discalced' Carmelites, for at that time the two still belonged to the same order. Fernandez worked in collaboration with Rubeo, but de Sargas decided to do without him. He was in favour of the 'discalced' but tactless in his zeal—he gave them posts in as many convents as possible so as to spread the reform, and, as he was anxious to have a reformed convent in his province, he gave to the 'discalced' the convent at San Juan del Puerto (Huelva) previously belonging to the 'calced'. Moreover he authorized many foundations—those of Seville, Granada and la Penuela—against Rubeo's wishes.

Soon the 'calced' Carmelites became worried and wanted to stop the spread of the 'discalced'. Before long it was no longer limitation that they were after, but outright suppression. The situation deteriorated so much that a meeting of the Spanish provincials was convoked. They obtained from the Pope the right to appoint apostolic commissioners themselves, a measure that should have calmed tempers and allowed of more flexibility, for commissioners appointed in this way would be more familiar with the internal susceptibilities of the order. But on hearing the news the apostolic nuncio negatived its effects by appointing the two former 'reforming' apostolic commissioners with even wider powers than they had had before. These measures produced indignation among the 'calced' Carmelites.

Tempers flared. Letters were sent to the King, Philip II, and the Pope.

In return two letters were sent to Teresa to demand an explanation, but they did not arrive in time, and as the 'discalced' were absent from the chapter held in Italy they were seen as rebels. Hence the suppression. It was decided to close the Andalusian convents which had been opened without Rubeo's permission, not to open any others, and to confine Teresa to a convent of her choice—it was forbidden for 'discalced' nuns to move from one convent to another.

But the 'calced' did not stop there. Early in 1576 they had captured John for the first time in his little house at the Incarnation and taken him as prisoner to Medina del Campo. But both the town and the nuncio had protested and John was returned to the Incarnation. But, profiting by the death of the nuncio favourable to the reform and confident of the support of his successor, a group of monks and laymen captured John again during the night of 2–3 December, 1577, and took him and his companion, Germán de San Matías, as prisoners to Carmel. They were beaten and locked up. Then John embarked on a foolhardy enterprise—he took advantage of a moment when his guards thought he was at mass to return to his house to dispose of his papers concerned with the reform. The result was that he and Germán were removed from Avila.

When Teresa was informed that John had been kidnapped she was deeply distressed and wrote twice to Philip II to beg him to intervene on John's behalf, but she did not know where he was. In fact he had been taken to the Carmelite monastery at Toledo, an imposing establishment housing 800 'calced' friars. He was brought before an ecclesiastical court and then locked up in the monastery prison for two months. After Germán had escaped, however, he was moved to another cell for greater security—it was dark and tiny and made specially for him. It was so cold that he developed frost–bite in his toes.

There he remained for nine months. He was deprived of all communication with the outside world, badly fed, without heating, unable to change his clothes. Sometimes monks came and spoke to him through the door, telling him with glee about the suppression of reformed convents and assuring him that he would never be let out. He was also told that he had tried to play the saint and had only succeeded in turning the order upside down. He began to doubt himself and all that he had done. What was more, there was no reason why Teresa and the other monks and nuns should not think that he had simply abandoned them.

At the end of six months his guard was changed. The new one was young and anxious to ease his prisoner's hardships. Whenever possible he tried to spare him the daily beating. At John's request he brought him a clean habit and writing materials. Thus it was that John could write down—when the light permitted—what he had started to compose in his head. It was here that he wrote a large part of *The Spiritual Canticle*, the *Romances* (in particular the one on the psalm 'By the waters of Babylon', which was appropriate in that it sings of the sorrows of exile), the poem,

How well I know the fount that freely flows
  Although 'tis night![1]

and probably, too, the poem of the *Dark Night*.

By August John was so weak that he thought he would die,

yet there was no question of setting him free. The 'calced' Carmelites were now in control of the 'discalced'. All he could do was to escape.

With the collusion of his jailer he discovered the lie of the land. Then he taught himself to open his cell without making a sound. Then he asked forgiveness of his jailer for getting him into trouble. Then he escaped by means of his bedclothes stitched and knotted together. After a sheer drop he leapt into the void, as his 'rope' was too short, and landed on an escarpment. Climbing over a roof, he arrived in the town where he found shelter for the rest of the night. In the morning he sought refuge with some Carmelite nuns.

Two months later (October 1578) the 'discalced' Carmelites called a chapter at Almodóvar which John attended though not yet recovered from his ordeal. Various decisions were taken. The 'discalced' Carmelites organized themselves on two fronts. In order to defend themselves from within they examined the directives given by Antonio of Jesus and John of the Cross at Duruelo, and those given by the Generals Soreth and Audet. Attention was paid to what was being done in the reformed convents of Castile and Andalusia, particularly regarding the relationship between the active and the contemplative life.

On the external front the members of the chapter, having been warned by Teresa of the accusations launched against the 'discalced', decided to dispatch an emissary to Rome to put their case to the Pope. The emissary was the superior of La Penuela, Pedro de los Angeles, and the aim was to negotiate the independence of the 'discalced' as the only way of saving the reform. A new provincial was appointed. John was made prior of the convent of Calvario to replace Nicolas Doria who was to be one of the mission to Rome.

The new nuncio, Sega, was informed of this chapter but refused to give it a sympathetic ear. He excommunicated all those who had taken part in it and imprisoned those under his control. And he put the 'discalced' Carmelites yet again under the jurisdiction of the 'calced'. As for Pedro de los Angeles, the principal envoy to Rome, he returned 'calced'.

However, in the summer of 1580 it was learned that on 22 June Pope Gregory XIII had ratified the separation between the 'calced' and the 'discalced'. Throughout the proceedings which resulted in that decision, King Philip II had sided with the 'discalced'. At last they could summon a chapter, the first, of their own order with the Pope's blessing, and this took place at Alcala de Henares. Its acts were signed on 15 March 1583, and John was one of the signatories.

So the 'discalced' Carmelites, no longer under the control of the 'calced', were now free to fight among themselves.

At their chapter held at Almodóvar on 1 May 1583, John was reproached for not visiting the laity enough and for bringing too little money into the congregation. He himself proposed the non–reelection of superiors and expressed disapproval at sending 'discalced' Carmelites as missionaries into parts of the country not yet ready for their austere way of life. None of his advice was followed, and he was sharply ordered back to his own duties.

On his way to Madrid in 1586 to attend a general chapter he fell ill in Toledo, but managed to reach his destination by 16 May. There, with Anne of Jesus, prioress of Granada, he opposed the provincial, Nicolas Doria, in his effort to make the 'discalced' Carmelites into an apostolic and centralized order. Contrary to what Teresa (who had died in 1582) would have wished, John did not want the Carmelite monasteries to be altogether independent from each other.

In June 1591 there was another general chapter in Madrid—for John yet another occasion for opposing Doria, this time regarding some nuns who wanted a 'discalced' superior and not to be under the control of the Consulta. John failed totally on this score, but agreed with Doria in his decision to remove him, John, from every office where he might be influential. Acting on John's own suggestion, Doria even thought of sending him to Mexico. But seeing that he now had nothing to fear from him, Doria decided to appoint him superior at Segovia. John turned down this post and went to La Penuela.

Here Diego Evangelista made use of his new office as 'definidor' to ill–treat and humiliate John and even bring a libel action against him: yes or no, had he been the lover of some of his female friends, Carmelite nuns in particular? During this time it seems that Doria, who was in Madrid, did not know what was going on.

It was now that John began to suffer from an infection of his right leg. Another monk, Hilarion, who was also ill, suggested that they should go to Baeza. John refused, saying he would go to Ubeda where no–one knew him. There he was kindly received by the monks, but the prior, Francisco Crisostomo, a harsh and severe man who had no liking for people who were regarded as saints, gave John, despite his physical weakness, the smallest and meanest cell.

John's condition grew worse. When the prior of La Penuela heard of Crisostomo's attitude, he sent corn and chickens to the convent to make up for the expenses incurred by the invalid's needs. When the nursing monk who tended him with loving care was replaced, he (the monk) wrote indignantly to the provincial, Antonio of Jesus, who arrived at the dying man's bedside and reinstated the nurse in his post.

John's condition grew worse. From 6 December he often asked the date. On the 7th he became weaker. The doctor decided that he should be told he was dying, and John received the news with joy. Many saints have endured terrible deaths, accompanied by total abandonment comparable to Christ's on the cross—'My God, my God, why has thou forsaken me?'[2] But John had lived in companionship with dereliction in the dark night of his captivity in 1578, so that the end, when it came, was comparatively gentle. On 11 December he asked for extreme unction. On the 12 December he asked for his papers to be burnt, almost all of them concerned with the libel action. On the 13 December he made peace with Crisostomo. Several times he asked what time it was and told the friars that he would warn them. By twelve o'clock all were with him. On 14 December, 1591, in the middle of the night, he died.

It is startling to observe how close was John's life to that of the Crucified. Like him, John was betrayed by those who should have defended his cause. Like him, John was attacked mainly by religious hierarchies, subjected to ecclesiastical proceedings and threatened with excommunication. He was betrayed at the heart of what served him as support—in the Church; and thus he was absolutely abandoned—except by God. But God was absent.

But we must not forget that John also experienced the full realization of love—he was the man of absolute Desire and of the success of Desire. His life reached out with all its might towards fulfilment, not suffering, and never colluded with failure in any lasting way. He always stubbornly strove towards what he had chosen. He yearned for plenitude, and the remarkable thing was that he also attained it.

CHAPTER THREE

I. Desire

If we want to grasp how a desiring relationship between the soul and God can exist, we must try to understand the nature of desire in all its diversity. But first it must be seen at work in the various stages of the mystical journey.

The *Ascent* shows the first stage as purifying the soul of its sensuality. This is a Platonic concept rather than a specifically Christian one: when the soul is 'purified' it is emptied of all that is not truly itself; it has trained itself to become detached from the body by renouncing belief in perception:

> In this first stanza the soul sings of the happy fortune and chance which it experienced in going forth from all things that are without, and from the desire and imperfections that are in the sensual part of man because of the disordered state of his reason.[1]

Here we have a definition of man, but we must look at it carefully before concluding that it represents John's whole thought; we must examine where it leads and whence it comes.

First point: the disorder reigning in the rational part of man brings with it a disorder of the senses. It is the disordered reason that disturbs the senses, not the senses that disturb the reason.

Second point: man is not invited to correct the disorder of the reason or the imperfections of the senses, but to 'go forth' from the sensory world, abandon it, leave it behind.

These two points give a simple and traditional view of man: man is made up of soul and body, his soul being superior to his body; he has to withdraw from his sensuality to re–establish a hierarchy that had been broken—the disorder of the reason being to concern itself with the sensory. One cannot but feel rather let down by this view. Contempt for the body, the assertion that body and soul are separate and distinct—surely this is a dead tradition and without biblical roots at that? The mortifications demanded by John are extremely dismal and very predictable.

Happily, this initial view cannot be upheld. At the beginning of the *Ascent* man is not defined just as a soul in a body. Something else comes into play, deriving from St Thomas Aquinas.[2] The relationship between the rational and sensory parts of man, between the soul and the body, is a relationship of love—and 'love creates a likeness between that which loves and that which is loved',[3] by which the lover becomes the beloved.

Still more characteristic of John, more original and closer to his thought, is the extraordinary image which he uses to illustrate what he is now trying to say:

And just as gold or diamond, if it were heated and placed upon pitch, would become foul and be stained by it, inasmuch as the heat would have cajoled and allured the pitch, even so the soul that is hot with desire for any creature draws forth foulness from it through the heat of its desire and is stained by it.[4]

So the soul is infinitely superior to the creature and should not for shame go stooping beneath itself. But how can we measure the distance between the two? Creatures are not evil as such but only as compared with the soul. True, John's vocabulary can mislead, for he sets it down in black and white that bodily creatures are less than nothing—they are mud:

And there is more difference between the soul and other corporeal creatures than between a liquid that is highly clarified and mud that is most foul.[5]

But his belittling of bodily creatures has a purpose, namely that attachment to them would preclude something else—union with God, the theme of his whole work. So now the violence of his vocabulary can be better understood. He does not insist that creatures should efface themselves as being vile and contemptible—this interpretation would not give them their true value. If God and the soul are infinitely superior to bodily creatures, it is not by belittling creatures but by valuing them that God and the soul are exalted. Creatures must be raised to the highest possible level if their insignificance is to show forth God's glory.

Our justification for putting forward this interpretation of John's thought is that creatures and the senses are later re–integrated into their dignity and glorified. This happens at the beginning of *The Spiritual Canticle* and from Book III onwards of the *Ascent*. John was, after all, a Christian. The conventions of his time probably influenced his vocabulary— every epoch stresses such and such an aspect that is in tune with its sensibility—but John's faith in the final glory of the body through the resurrection preserved the essentials of his religion.

In any case the creature's status (in his thought) is lowly only as compared with God. In the passages under discussion his tone is depreciatory, but he is not referring to the creature, or the soul, but to the defiling of the soul 'that clings to creatures'.[6] The soul has the power to pervert reality and to be perverted by it. The appetite is here envisaged as a force that makes creatures unreal, that consumes them, absorbs them, instead of letting them be *other* in their freedom and independence. That is to say, there exists in man a power of desiring that perverts, not because it turns to something evil, but because it isolates. In the *Ascent* man is characterized above all by appetite (*apetito*). This is not a form of desire that lifts man out of himself, but one that encloses him in himself and cuts him off from the rest of the universe. It is an attitude similar to the one described by E. Lévinas in *Totalité et Infini*: the soul settles down in its desire so finds itself in the same position of dependence as creatures, it finds itself in a state of isolation, of folding–in on itself, or self–sufficiency; the soul can say, 'to be myself, to be a non–believer, to be at home, to be self–sufficient, to be happy, to be created—these are all the same thing'.[7]

The soul as here described knows nothing of the other— not only the human other, and not only through egoism. More seriously, it does not know the category of otherness. It does not know that otherness exists, something other than itself, not less than itself. Not knowing about the other, it can only talk, see and experience the Same. And yet the soul is nothing if not a yearning of the appetite for the other. The soul is ignorant of otherness and yet otherness shapes it. Its yearning exhausts itself in its effort to reject the clinging embrace of the world.

At the beginning of the *Ascent* man is ensnared in his sensual attitudes but is not yet a disordered being; he desires but does not know what he desires; he does not know that he desires the other. This is the desire that John calls appetite—it sees its object only as something to devour. The soul must be led along paths that will prevent it from settling down in the atheism of appetite. Man must be taught to avoid living as a being of appetite. Appetite is not man's truth but his first error. He should therefore clothe himself in an active rejection of the temporal:

> Strive always to choose, not that which is easiest, but that which is most difficult;
> Not that which is most delectable, but that which is most unpleasing;
> Not that which gives most pleasure, but rather that which gives least;
> Not that which is restful, but that which is wearisome;
> Not that which gives consolation, but rather that which makes disconsolate;
> Not that which is greatest, but that which is least;
> Not that which is loftiest, and most precious, but that which is lowest and most despised;
> Not that which is a desire for anything, but that which is a desire for nothing;
> Strive not to go about seeking the best of temporal things, but the worst.
> Strive thus to desire to enter into complete detachment and emptiness and poverty with respect to that which is in the world, for Christ's sake.[8]

What is true for man's sensual part is also true for the spiritual:

> In this second stanza the soul sings of the happy chance which it experienced in stripping the spirit of all spiritual

imperfections and desires for the possession of spiritual things.[9]

The process suggested here is exactly parallel to the previous one. It deals with escaping from the spirit of possession, from appetite in the spiritual domain. The only difference is that here the appetite is not directly linked to the body.

It is here that John introduces the image of the transparent window quoted above.[10] By detaching itself from all possessions the spirit becomes transparent. It no longer conceals its master, God within it. God's being must be allowed to show itself in man. Man strips himself to the point of becoming transparent and lets God's possession of him shine through. Each of his dimensions will be stripped naked so that God's presence may be seen in each.

Man is revealed as God's image—the will is charity, the intelligence is faith, the memory is hope. This requires intense activity on the believer's part. He must make himself make the huge effort to want nothing, to strip himself of himself. But as this is his way of letting God show through, a spectacular reversal will take place. Up till now the believer has been active, but now that he is seeking to let God show in him and through him, the believer must be silent so as to hear God's silence. He must become passive.

The actions employed by the soul to denude itself have now passed into nature, they have become the soul's very being, hidden in the depths of its being so that they cannot see themselves, nor do they know they are doing this. There is no self–vision at the practical level (example: I don't know *how* I manage my body, I just manage it, full stop). In this sense it is possible to say that inward training tends to become a passivity, it hides man from his own eyes. But the activity of denudation is God; hence man hides God within him. There is nothing more to be seen, as when a ray of sunlight becomes invisible as soon as the dust dancing in the air disappears.

So there is a darkness that is brightness at the very heart of man, man's centre is absolutely transparent, that is to say, empty. Man is divinized or divinizable because he is holed, pierced. The fact that God can take possession of him shows him that his centre is that dark ray that lights up everything in its path. This stage of the journey is very interesting—it charts how man contains his own transcendence within him by a method both familiar and foreign. Man carries within himself his empty centre, and it is into this emptiness that God plunges:

> for the enamoured soul finds that that which is natural has failed it, and it is then imbued with that which is Divine, both naturally and supernaturally, so that there may be no vacuum in its nature.[11]

To understand this image we must remember that, in John's view, God is present to man in two ways, as his creator and as the object of his love. The possibility of mysticism is based on the second way. Man's retreat will allow God to show himself because he is already there. To make the emptiness is to aspire, but here it is the emptiness that aspires. So man's retreat certainly makes room for God, but God's part does not expand according to its strength but in answer to a call. There is no such thing as imperialism with God. There is the call of emptiness, of nothingness. It is a way of saying that God is more myself than I am.

God expands in man because of man's emptiness. That is to say, it is not exactly a purification that accounts for God in man, a purification does not create emptiness, it is not aspirational. For man to embrace this aspiration he must join up with his empty centre, rest there passively, and this is his passivity. He must do *nothing*. But as this is difficult, he has the power to be absorbed into his centre and hide himself there. The fact of leaving the centre absolutely alone is what brings it silence.

God is man's silence. The silent man divinizes himself. Man's being is silence. Consequently in his acceptance of God's will be has to reject everything else: nothing can enter this silent and tranquil zone. Man, the being of 'yes', can only say 'no'. John looks at all the forms of communication with God, whether illusory or not, and to all of them he says 'no'.[12] This rejection applies to everything that can come from God in the name of God. So it is not only centred on man (nothing in man should be like God) but also on God (no manifestation of God is God).

So we witness another reversal. Once man has reached this

extreme desolation, this arid desert, the world comes back
into his life, but strangely purified. God has unfolded himself
within man's emptiness, and now creatures are going to
appear in God's emptiness in man. Though they will again
be rejected, they will reappear in all their goodness, and here
John shows great tenderness for created things,

> he will find greater joy and recreation in the creatures
> through his detachment from them, for he cannot rejoice
> in them if he look upon them with attachment to them as
> to his own.[13]

Thus man is only really himself when denuded, he only fulfils
himself in the act of detachment. Then we see that joy can
result from the rejection of creatures; through rejection, man
becomes happy,

> as the Saviour says, they shall receive an hundredfold in
> this life,[14] so that, if thou deniest thyself one joy, the Lord
> will give thee an hundredfold in this life, both spiritually
> and temporally; and likewise, for one joy that thou hast in
> these things of sense, thou shalt have an hundredfold of
> affliction and misery.[15]

It is not easy to interpret this passage, but one suggestion
at least can be eliminated, namely that joys are rejected
through a fear of life. If this were so John would stress the
dangers of the joy that entails 'an hundredfold of affliction'.
Such an attitude would represent a flight into the imaginary—
since pleasure rejected but still savoured is an imaginary
pleasure. So we would have to agree that the imaginary is
preferable to, and affords more joy than, the real. But everything discussed in this book, where the reality of the journey
is shown as one of its main features, belies such an interpretation. John did not reject life, if he had his courage in face of
the dark night would be incomprehensible. Nor was there any
morose delectation where he was concerned, no narcissistic
dwelling on the renunciation of pleasures. Pleasures were not
rejected for themselves or how could other and more numer-
ous pleasures be won through their rejection? John did not
try to gloss over the gospel texts—we really are dealing with
joy or pleasure, with possessions and the here–below.

A second interpretation seems much less false than false

asceticism. It is based on the time factor: a man rejects a pleasure in the knowledge that a hundred others will come to him, on some other occasion, at some other moment in his life, and not at all because he wants to reject this particular pleasure.

But the expectation of pleasure coming from God in the ordinary course of life presents problems, for what could be more contradictory than seeing a pleasure as good yet repeatedly rejecting it? Something interesting and legitimate can emerge from this way of seeing things, however. A vision of life as a succession of events over which we have no control but holding all sorts of delectable adventures in store for us, is not at all an unacceptable one.

The way whereby we make ourselves owners (or not) of the present is the way whereby we close ourselves (or not) to the future. But, and this is the essential point, the act of owning something is an act that denies time. By saying that such an object, or such an event, or such a joy, is *mine*, I imply that it will always be mine, that time will have no hold over my ownership. On the other hand to let my ownership be taken from me now, by an upheaval of events within time, is more than renouncing a series of particular things, of pleasures, for instance. It is to be dispossessed of myself. Thus to renounce pleasures is to renounce myself by consenting to the flow of time.

Detachment from the self, ceasing to hold by the self, implies also the capacity to see something other than the self, to know that other beings exist. The rejection of possessions brings man a lucidity that lies at the source of joy and enables him to perceive a multiplicity of realities. But the 'recreation in creatures' brings a unique joy. Indeed there is but one joy—the joy that God exists. Everything, down to the humblest creature, speaks of God to the man who has melted his own hard heart through possessing nothing.

> There comes to the soul a spiritual joy, directed to God in all things that are seen, whether Divine or profane.[16]

The *Ascent* finishes at the point where man has acquired an infinite love and respect for creatures and has understood that this arises from an absolute preference for God. But we must follow this through to its conclusion, for to prefer God to ourselves does not mean that we can settle down in this preference and in some way appropriate God. Those who have reached the top of the *Ascent* know that they must step back from this relationship with God—they must love God so much that they love God and God only, not the privileged relationship with him. The distinction is subtle but important, for when God is loved above everything he is loved more than any possible appropriation of him. The process of denudation has then become complete. Man has settled down outside himself, so he is not self–sufficient. The words happy, self–sufficient, non–believing cease to be synonymous when the words happy, non–self–sufficient, believing, become synonymous in their turn.

After the *Ascent*, the *Dark Night*. The same poem is used for the *Dark Night*, but the commentary is different. Here it is not man's self–denudation that is at issue, but his passivity once denuded of everything; not *his* activity of shedding his encumbrances, but *God's* activity upon him. While pursuing his ascent through the dark night man discovers who he is, but he discovers it better and more inwardly. The same and yet transformed, he repeats the *Ascent*, but now it would be true to say that he has entered the native land of truth.

John gives a name to man's privileged relationship with truth—humility. The *Dark Night* finds the believer at the point where the *Ascent* left him. Though much advanced—for now he lets God dwell in him—he is not without faults. A secret pride at having arrived this far hampers the flexibility required for following the Spirit. The tribulations of the *Dark Night* are intended to break down this pride so that perfection may be reached. So now the believer will despise himself, for all those who reach perfection rejoice in being the least of men:

> holding themselves as of little worth, they are anxious that others too should thus hold them, and should despise and depreciate that which they do. And further, if men should praise and esteem them, they can in no wise believe what they say; it seems to them strange that anyone should say these good things of them.[17]

Contempt has a bad press, and this is understandable. As for self-contempt and, worse still, taking pleasure in self–

contempt, these are still more suspect. They belong to neurosis. At best, and in order to spare John an interpretation along pathological lines, it is tempting to view the last quotation as an exaggeration.

But this would miss the point. To get back to the rudiments: the humble man does not rejoice in his lowliness as such, he rejoices in his correct assessment of himself; it is not being the least or the lowest that makes him happy, but being alive to the truth. But I can only rejoice at being right if I love myself. If I hate myself, what does it matter whether I'm right or wrong? If I rejoice in being right, where is my joy rooted if not in myself? So, having dismissed an interpretation of John along pathological lines, we can now face a second objection—that this humility is a false humility, concealing pride.

In fact the humble man knows what he wants—not a lot—but he can love himself because he loves the truth and has placed his happiness not in himself but in the truth. With the result that in a way he becomes the truth—loving the truth, he becomes the truth. And if he rejoices that others are better than he is, it is not because he has illusions about others, or because he is overflowing with generosity, but because, by knowing that he is the least, he has eliminated all standards of comparison, he no longer compares but sees everyone just as themselves. He does not experience himself as the least of men but as a man freed from all standards of comparison with anyone else. His humility is thus not a guarantee against error but a liberation of himself. Freed from himself, he is ready to take any path, even the most improbable, even the most unthinkable, even the path that the Spirit of God wants for him:

> with great tranquillity and humbleness, these souls are very ready to travel and set out on another road than that which they are actually following, if they be so commanded, because they never think that they are right in anything whatsoever.[18]

So the man whom the *Dark Night* wants to reach does not value himself. He is ready to set off anywhere because he has no inner rules. By the same token he is not subject to any law but his own. Indeed he is in the highest imaginable state of freedom because God alone is guiding him, guiding him by his hidden interiority. Perfection has taught him his inner emptiness, so he has learnt, not merely his nothingness, but his basic (and liberating) dependence resulting from this. But how can dependence be liberating? it may be asked. Because it is produced by the free gift of our being. Our being (the fact that we exist) has no definable origin—it has been given to us. Given. Our being is dependent because we do not make ourselves. But *being* is freedom itself. It depends on itself alone, for what would it depend on otherwise? The perfect man thus discovers that he has received himself as a free gift, so that for him all is grace.

According to John, this man has God as his centre. But God cannot be seen to be man's centre. If God were seen to be man's centre, if God were found in man, then man's being would cease to be autonomous, it would cease to be free. Man must in some way be reduced to size, separated from God, if he is to be truly given to himself, and given freely. So what of God is seen in the believer? Nothing. God's visible reality in the believer will be that which is not God, that is to say, evil.

We never see what we are. We only see what is far enough away to be seen. The believer is too close to the free gift of his being to be able to see it. But he sees very well what he has rejected and what is moving away from him, evil.

This passage is dramatic. In fact it is only here that the dark night really begins. The believer sees nothing at all, he is like an owl that cannot see the light of day. This is a terrible purgation in which the soul feels itself to be at war with God. Man then becomes engulfed in his own secret, in the battle between the visible which he believes he is, and the invisible which he is without knowing it. This is not the moment to speak to God, it is the moment to enter into silent suffering. Then, in the silence of the night, love can show itself and the night comes to an end. These are the last words of the *Dark Night*:

yet its [the soul's] love alone, which burns at this time, and makes its heart to long for the Beloved, is that which now moves and guides it, and makes it soar upward to its God along the road of solitude, without its knowing how or in what manner.[19]

The work is unfinished, the commentary is incomplete, but the *Dark Night* continues in the *Spiritual Canticle*.

The starting–point of the *Spiritual Canticle* is the Beloved's absence. Wounded by love, the soul has gone out from itself to try to find the One who has bruised it. But the Beloved has already gone. Whence the cries of the soul that has loosed itself from all things so as to reach the Beloved, and now finds itself deprived of everything, even of what it had gained.

This is where the soul sets out on an unexpected venture. In its despair, it sets out to meet the world, to meet creation, but creation reflects the creator and so increases the soul's love. Thus the Beloved's absence produces a yearning for God inspired by the beauty of the world. Each and every created thing takes on a value which, at one and the same time, leaves the creature in insignificance (it's only a creature after all, nothing compared with God), rejects the ordering of the world as a substitute for God (this would be pantheism, which holds that the world is God), and yet endows nature (and the beings that people it) with a beauty befitting the glory of God. Here we see a remarkable and rare balance between the exaltation of nature and the rejection of pantheism. It is in fact the rejection of pantheism that acknowledges and guarantees the value proper to the creature (it is a created being, distinct from God). True, this thinking is not specific to John; it is very close to what St Augustine was writing at the dawn of the fifth century:

> I spoke to all the things that are about me, all that can be admitted by the door of the senses, and I said, 'Since you are not my God, tell me about him. Tell me something of my God'. Clear and loud they answered, 'God is he who made us'. I asked these questions simply by gazing at these things, and their beauty was all the answer they gave.[20]

John's great originality, however, was to show that here we have a premonition of death.

Since the soul has been denied the object of its love—except for the reflections of him to be found in created things—its only contact with the Beloved is its love for him, that is to say its yearning for him and hence its separation from him. This being so, the soul can only hope for a tremendous increase of its love to make good the separation by something that tells of it—in other words, the separation.

As a result the entire soul becomes love. But given the way this increase of love has come about, the soul is again separated from its goal. So man both gets and does not get what he is seeking. On the one hand man is love of God, but God is love, so man is God. On the other hand God is given only in love, hence a yearning that does not reach its goal of total fusion and union. It should be seen that this limitation of love is both able and unable to be overreached, like all moments of mysticism, and that it is within the absent relationship that God is found. Indeed, faced with the yearning love that has invaded the believer's whole being, the Beloved's arrival will not be delayed; but he will come in the measure that he remains absent. And now the soul will cry out, because of the extraordinary depths of its yearning—not with an inarticulate cry but one of wonderful precision:

And let the vision of thee and thy beauty slay me.[21]

We must try to measure how much self–renunciation, how much taste for death and suffering are contained in the 'beauty' referred to in that line. We must also try to see death not as something to be undergone but as an act of contemplation. True, 'and let the vision of thee and thy beauty slay me' then means 'let me pass into the other world, where you are'; but the demand is urgent and brings with it a parallel demand: 'Change me into what I am, nothing, for I am but the absence of you'. Now this is not death but faith. So the soul must settle down within God's absence as though within God himself. In other words, death is indeed offered to the soul, but there where death resides—in the future. That is the hope that bestows on the soul the unseen promise of a life in God.

Strengthened by this assurance, and choosing this as the perfect moment, the soul takes flight outside the flesh. It will try to disincarnate itself, for death is a disincarnation, or so it is said. But this is a snare and a pitfall, for disincarnation is not what love offers; no, the soul will find itself led back to its body, this being the true site of love. So the soul takes flight outside the flesh, but the Beloved calls it back—he, too, has a body and a wounded body, they have a common wound to tend. Thus John re–introduces the body at the least expected moment.

The soul must know that it is incarnate, because the Beloved himself is incarnate. So we see how the flight outside the body, as described in the *Ascent*, cannot possibly be interpreted as a denial of the body or a wish to separate the soul from the body, so as to install man in his soul (and a believing one, if possible!). Quite the reverse—inasmuch as the movement of flight is genuine, it *has to* lead back to the body.

There follows the spiritual betrothal: 'the torrent of the Spirit of God' assails the soul[22] while showing it the depths of its hollow places. God's voice re–echoes within it though adapting itself to the soul's weakness—whence the 'silent music' to which the soul now finds itself peacefully summoned. Man has been broken, he has learnt that his life is a life for God, and that outside God nothing really is, not even himself. So he comes to the spiritual marriage, where everything that is not God is forgotten. He has only one activity, for henceforth even his first movements conform to God's will—

For now my exercise is in loving alone.[23]

Now the soul is truly lost to all things—only God looks at it and loves it.

But this is not the end. The ascent must go on. God loves only himself, so he raises up the soul until it is lovable for him and he may be captivated and entranced by it. The infinite peace which then sets in is not the peace of satiation. The soul burns sweetly because there is nothing to burn within it unless it be God himself. Then the humble sensory part can come and share in the union.

The divine union is the subject of the *Living Flame*. The soul described by John here is 'enkindled' by God's love, each of God's movements being also a movement of the soul.[24] The same flame that purified before now burns and enkindles the soul. It sears everything it meets, even the wounds; it changes everything into itself. The soul dwells in the flame like air within fire—it cannot be seen. God takes the soul under his shadow, the soul *is* God's shadow. These metaphors are

John's attempt to show how God and the soul can be one though without forming one being. At the heart of the oneness the soul experiences God only in the emptiness that is within it to receive him. Any other desire for God is not turned to God.

At the pinnacle of mysticism is found a relationship of mutual respect—the soul lets God be and God lets the soul be. Then it can be said that God dwells away from the soul and yet within it, just as the soul is in God yet separated from him. This is what John is expressing when he writes that God, so as not to break the soul, dwells in it secretly, so secretly that he is felt by the soul to be hardly stirring when he effects 'delectable awakenings' within it.[25] Henceforth man is wholly God's and wholly reality's, wholly God's and wholly human, with a soul restored to itself and snatched from itself in the same process.

With the *Living Flame* the journey started in the *Ascent* comes to an end. We have tried to chart its course to show what it says about man, John's idea of man. We already knew that in John's scheme desire lies at man's centre, but we are now perhaps in a better position to see how and why.

This is the point at which to ponder the questions that seem so crucial to John and to us. The purpose is not to betray his thought or interpret it fancifully but, rather than comment on it as such, to develop our own thoughts around it, thoughts which could not exist without his as inspiration.

The general impression that emerges from reading John's works is that of man's diversity and unity. Man's diversity is well charted by the various definitions of him: composed of soul and body, a creature of appetite, transparent, empty, silent, dispossessed, not self–sufficient, not valuing himself, a 'yes' being, a being of love. His unity is no less variously defined, and it is this that concerns us now—we must ponder the unity of this diversity, try to dispense with the journey as the way of showing what man is. But the journey occupies such a large place in John's work that it cannot simply be dismissed; what one has to do is show that man's passage from one stage to the next, from one configuration to the next, is brought about by desire, and it must be shown that this is the way desire works—all the stages and configurations inter–relate through the yearning that animates them; there has to be yearning for the Other in order that one stage may become the next.

This, according to John, is the role and definition of desire: to be open to what is not myself through the attraction of its very difference; to bring forth from myself a thing that was absent before which polarizes what I have experienced and what I am going to experience.

As the notion of desire is the keystone of any description of the believer, we must explor its meaning as deeply as we can and thus add to the philosophy of the man of mystical 'experience'.

So what is desire? The notion is ambiguous. The most obvious form under which we meet it is that of need. Need is an emptiness, it is a call for satisfaction to another than myself. This is at its most obvious in the matter of food. When I need to eat I turn towards what is not me (food) so as to change it into myself (my body). Need makes the body open to that which will become the body. But this is not all. The next point is that we cannot give ourselves the object of our need—we have to encounter it. Similarly we do not give ourselves our needs from without, we have to encounter them from within. Need is thus the part of ourselves that goes out to meet the real so as to devour it—a part of ourselves that is both deeper and simpler than we are. But this part of ourselves recognizes the real only under the form of lack, and it dies of satisfaction as soon as the real has been encountered. So need gives us nothing—it hands us over to the real, it does not give the real to us. As much as to say that need, of itself, knows nothing of satisfaction. As regards such simple things as hunger and thirst, it can only give us a promise that we shall never hunger or thirst again. Need is the absent presence of the real within us.

So need cannot go outside itself despite its requirements— we were hoping for openness but it remains closed. This is why man cannot *need* the other. If need can symbolize the relationship with God by showing a type of dependence on God which has nothing to do with the domain of the soul, then it will remain a symbol. True need has to destroy and assimilate its object. To need God would mean to destroy and assimilate him. Need needs the other, but not the otherness of the other.

And yet we cannot do without need. To get rid of it, to say it is not part of desire, would deny the body, and it is through the body that we know that desire is not confined to just knowing. So we must go right to the centre of need, where its function is to assimilate, and see how this can be transfigured by desire. The main obstacle is that assimilation destroys the otherness of the other. For need to be corrected so that it leads to desire, it does not have to be denied for this would only disguise the difficulty. As need cannot cease to devour the otherness of the other, it must itself be devoured by its object. Not that need for another necessarily implies possessing and devouring it. It is in its own inwardness as need, in the movement that leads it towards its object, that the other should destroy it. It is not that another should devour me, but that I should be seized by the other in the very act that makes me want to take possession of it. This is reciprocity. Transfigured by reciprocity, need becomes love. In love I make my way towards the other but find myself possessed by him instead of possessing him.

But reciprocity cannot be brought to the inwardness of need unless another dimension is introduced. We must show need its emptiness if it is to cease to be itself and become what we are looking for, and we must also show it its un-reality; so the change of need into desire presupposes the unreal—that is, the imagination.

It is on the plane of the imagination that need can raise itself to desire. But imagination is not the truth of desire, for to imagine is to see what is not there. I cannot *imagine* what I see in front of me; short of turning away my head, or shutting my eyes, or inventing a situation, I cannot imagine what I am actually looking at. Moreover—and here lies the charm of all images—the image gives me what I want as if I already possessed it. I cannot imagine an object, and desire it, without imagining that I possess it. In other words, some-thing I can only imagine in association with possessing it becomes something I desire. But the imagination cannot give more than it has. I cannot grasp the being it imagines. Per-haps all we know of beings we have learnt from images rather than from reality, but reality never seems real in the imagi-nary world. The imagination shows forth—excellently and in depth—but it does not take possession. But as it imagines possession, possession interests it—hence its disappointment when it reaches its goal and reality is given to it. It then sees that this was not what it wanted; or rather, when it meets its object it too disappears—sometimes in a burst of joy.

Neither need nor imagination achieve what they want. Desire is deceptive. All that desire can say when trying to rise above need and imagination is: what I am seeking is elsewhere.

This is the meaning of all consolation offered to desire. Any effort to console desire for being unable to satisfy itself lies in reminding it that other things exist, in turning it towards other objects than the one seen by the imagination. So we send desire back to need ('it doesn't matter if you haven't got *this* because you've got all the rest to choose from'). And we shall also remind need of how vain her satisfaction is ('if you had had what you wanted, what would you have gained?'). These consoling remarks have only the value that they have. In fact they are contradictory and encourage suicide in a universal, 'what's the use?'. They say very little except that the answer to desire lies elsewhere. 'Desire is deceptive because it is never fulfilled'. Such is the mournful litany of a despairing wisdom.

Yet these commonplace remarks do point to something very true, namely that desire remains alive only if it is beyond what is seen and assimilated. Desire does not and cannot know what its object is.

But this is a reason for happiness, not despair. The desired 'elsewhere' is not an object—it is the supremely desirable, separated from all objects. Our examination of desire has taught us the meaning of the word Absolute, which does not, however, mean that the Absolute exists for that reason.

At the same time we have learnt that desire is vague regarding the Absolute—it can see the Absolute as anything whatever and anything whatever as the Absolute. Even nothingness, even death can be given a meaning and be used to symbolize the totality of meaning in the universe. Desire can teach us nothing but its ignorance of the Absolute; in no way can it tell us anything about it, not even whether it exists.

And yet it is desire that is at issue in the relationship with the Absolute. By its very failure to define the Absolute it shows that it recognizes the Absolute for what it is, namely

Other. If the Absolute exists, it is only to desire that it will disclose itself, for only desire (among human agents) can produce such a disclosure. As soon as something in man betrays his wish for the Absolute Other and his own inability to provide it, this something is desire.

So desire finds its true place. Its basic incapacity is not a sign of weakness, still less a disqualification. But it has a price to pay—it has no inner truth, all its meaning comes from its 'elsewhere', from the Absolute. The truth of desire changes according to what is, or is not, the Absolute.

But if desire is determined from outside while being the only means of access to the Absolute, then it becomes impossible to speak of the Absolute. The only way the Absolute could remove its incognito would be by speaking to desire. If desire were spoken to by the Absolute (supposing it exists, and is capable of speaking, and decides to do so) then desire in its turn could speak its fill about itself and the Absolute. But desire would not have jurisdiction over what it says, indeed it would have to start by saying that its meaning and its truth have been bestowed on it.

If the Absolute were to speak, its words would reach to the inmost depths of desire. But the truth, coming to desire from outside, would convulse it without changing it, without interrupting its course between need and imagination. Desire would still need, would still imagine, but would never be able to imagine the Absolute, or need to.

Two comments can be made about this.

First, in any situation, man is separated from the Absolute, otherwise the Absolute would not be the Absolute—not because it has to be transcendent, but because man can only desire what is distant. This does not mean that proximity would sully the Absolute, but that desire can only exist if distant from its object, so only distance allows a union between desire and the Absolute, between man and the Absolute.

Man is in a sense abandoned to himself in any event, especially if the Absolute exists and if he finds himself at a desiring distance from it. For it is when man has a relationship with the Absolute, not when he hasn't, that his abandonment is thinkable. Just as the idea of death is no more terrible to the non–believer, though he lacks 'consolation', than to the believer, though he has it, so here it is not the non–believer who is conscious of man's abandonment (*by whom* would he be abandoned?) but the believer. Only within belief can a separation of this kind be envisaged, for, without belief, it could not be sustained except by magic. The gap would close with the proposition: everything is natural, man and his death included.

The second point is that this concept of man involves no special pleading. Indeed it respects two seemingly opposed requirements, (1) that it should not be seen as a neutral description with everything on the same plane; and (2) that all man's described attitudes should be genuinely possible. A concept of man based on desire should be possible even if the non–believer is right; in other words, desire need not know its object so should be seen as neutral regarding belief. Thus we must look at the desiring man in the context of the non–existence of the Absolute.

He would have to reject the existence of the Absolute so as to restore desire to its true place. This would not mean the collapse of desire but a change in its truth—its concern with 'elsewhere' would remain but, as 'elsewhere' would not exist, it would become its own 'elsewhere'. Man would then embark on a huge task, but not the task of dreaming–up a non–believer's mysticism. True, such a possibility exists; he would find a place for 'elsewhere' and then abolish it, in other words nothingness would replace the Absolute. In this case the non–believing process would appoint itself as sole effective agent to criticize belief. No, if we are serious about the absence of the Absolute, something else is needed for thinking the truth of man.

The imaginary, not controlled by the Word of the Absolute, would tend to spread out in all directions, but would at once be rejected by non–imaginary activity. So a constant post-ponement of make–believe would result. This would be brought about by a pre–eminently non–make–believe activity—science. Science escapes from the imaginary only through its inner rules, but the rigorous processes which should pre-serve it intact are never completed. Science is for ever upset-ting its own bases through its discoveries even in areas as 'transparent' as mathematics. The developments of science do not close, but open, its field of action.

So desire's 'elsewhere' becomes time or history: *later* the imaginary shall be destroyed. This is not an illusion but a brave undertaking involving the constant postponement of the moment when it can be said, 'this is definitively true'. In the act of postponement lies the process that begets truth.

So the action of desire is wholly preserved, and atheism— that is, the absence of the Absolute as the object of desire— can be envisaged in a concept of man that places desire at man's centre. Man can aspire to the other–than–himself, and even if this turns out to be illusory, he can eliminate the illusion without changing the structure.

A concept of man as a creature of desire has now been established. It remains to consider what it means to 'desire God'.

II. John of the Cross—a Being of Desire

Only God is desirable. Only the Absolute, once it has spoken, can lay the foundations of desire in itself. With John the fulfilment of desire takes place through his relationship with God. So he loves only God. Of course creatures make their way back into his life, but very much as creatures rather than as human beings. On the whole his work shows a negative attitude to human relationships. References to them tend to stress how they should *not* be treated: behave as though the community does *not* exist; do *not* judge others whether for good or bad, and so on.

This is not really surprising although it is obvious that there is another side to the picture. Yet even here God and God alone is the mediator. The question, 'What about the possibility of loving our neighbour?' remains unanswered.

Yet the question is crucial. Two remarks should be made about it, (1) in pointing out the lack of texts on the subject, it should be remembered how John wrote and for whom he was writing; (2) there is John's own life to consider—what were his friendships and his relationships with others? So we are not working in a void. We have sufficient material to begin to answer the question.

True, only a comprehensive history of mankind would en- able us to come to a conclusion about love of God and love of neighbour and the connection between them.[1] But in the pages that follow it will at least be possible to make a study of John's contribution to the subject, with the help and guidance of the well–known statement of John the Evangelist, 'for he who does not love his brother whom he has seen cannot love God whom he has not seen'.[2]

To go back to the beginning: love of God has absolute priority over love of brother. In John's view we do not ascend from creatures up to God (unless it be by rejecting them) but it is possible to descend from God down to creatures. Thus Love is at the origin of our capacity to love something else than love itself. In other words, God's love for me makes possible my love for my brothers. John indicated his criterion for the rightness of this love as follows: if loving creatures increased his love for God,[3] if the more he loved God the more he loved creatures and the more he loved creatures the more he loved God. If it were not like this, if the loves ran equally side by side, then one would find itself in opposition to the other. I could not love God *and* creation; whoever loved the one would hate the other.

John's life was punctuated by his friendships—perhaps essentially three.

The first was with Teresa of Avila. On 14 August 1567 she arrived at Medina del Campo to found her second convent of 'discalced' Carmelite nuns. She was aged fifty–two, very lively and ready to make jokes, and with a strong personality. With few exceptions, everyone was hostile to her project yet, far from being discouraged by this disapproval, she dreamed of extending the project and reforming the Carmelite friars too. So off she went to find an ally among them, one capable of carrying out what she wanted to initiate. Fr Antonio of Jesus, prior at Medina del Campo, and a supporter of Teresa, told her about John who at that time was still known by his first name as a religious, John of St Matthew. She met him in September of that year. The interview filled her with joy and affection for the man whom she called 'her little Seneca'. John was only five foot tall. She said she had 'a friar and a half' on her side—Antonio of Jesus and John of St Matthew.

John began his activity as a 'discalced' Carmelite at Duruelo. On 9 August he accompanied Teresa to the foundation of Rio de Olmos (Valladolid). In March 1569 Teresa visited

Duruelo, where she saw John at work, and very well he succeeded there. Not long after she decided he would be useful at Pastrana. The decision to let him go was made by Fr Antonio in mid–October 1570, and John set out immediately.

At the end of 1572 he went to the Incarnation at Avila, where Teresa was prioress. He stayed there for two years in a mutual trust and collaboration that never wavered. Teresa wrote that they were not always in agreement, but, as she had put it in a letter in 1568, 'I was the sole cause' of any friction. He was not under her domination, he knew how to stand up for himself, and he scrupulously watched over the spiritual development of his remarkable penitent.[4] They were very independent of each other, even in their attitudes to the spiritual life. Teresa's writings do not necessarily accord with John's, and a careful study would be required to chart their points of unity.

In 1574 John accompanied Teresa to the founding of the convent (of nuns) at Segovia which took place on 18 March.

In the summer of 1574 the chapter at Alcala de Henares took place. Five months later John went to Castile and took the opportunity to visit Teresa at Avila to persuade her to found a new convent at Granada (13 November 1581). Teresa, aged sixty–six, was tired and had already promised to go to Burgos. However, she selected some nuns to go to Granada with John while she sadly remained in Avila. The two never met again. Teresa died in 1582.

John's second friendship was with Anne of Jesus. John met her for the first time at Mancera in November 1570. She was then a young novice. It was only later that they formed a deep friendship. At first Anne of Jesus was anything but enthusiastic about him and, to Teresa's amazement, complained at not having a better confessor! But when John set off for the foundation at Granada in 1581, Anne of Jesus was of the party. They arrived at Beas on 8 December and set off again on 15 January 1582 despite an appalling storm and the fact that Anne was ill. On their arrival at Granada they could find neither the house they were looking for nor permission to install themselves anywhere, but only a hostile archbishop—though a frightened and remarkably mollified one due to the lightning that had just struck the episcopal palace.

The foundation took place and Anne of Jesus was the prioress. As for John, he was elected prior in the same town, at the convent of the Martyrs which the Carmelites had occupied for the past nine years. It was there that he finished the *Ascent*, and, at the request of Anne of Jesus, wrote the *Dark Night*. Finally he wrote the *Spiritual Canticle*, following on from what he had already written in prison in 1578. The title of this work is a tribute to his friendship with Anne:

Spiritual Canticle
exposición of the stanzas which treat of the exercise of love between the Soul and Christ the Spouse, wherein are touched upon and expounded some points and effects of prayer, at the request of Mother Ana de Jesús, Prioress of the Discalced at San José of Granada. The year 1584.

Of course the poem and its commentary were written as a dialogue between Christ and the soul. But in writing them John was also thinking of a particular person, one of his friends, discreetly present from one end of the text to the other, written for her and, in a sense, by her. Their whole relationship is there, though mediated by the relationship of each with God and their concern for God's love.

Later, in 1586, Anne of Jesus was transferred to Madrid.

John's third friendship was with Anne of Penalosa. The two first met in 1582, when John and Anne of Jesus and the other nuns chosen by Teresa arrived at Granada and were finally taken in and given hospitality by a widow belonging to the nobility. This was Anne of Penalosa.

Once installed as prior at the convent of the Martyrs, John wrote the *Living Flame* for, and at the request of, Anne of Penalosa. Here, too, the dedication is noteworthy. This time the friend is mentioned not only in the title but in the prologue to the work:

I have felt some unwillingness, most noble and devout lady, to expound these four stanzas which your Honour has requested me to explain, for they relate to things so interior and spiritual that words commonly fail to describe them, since spirit transcends sense and it is with difficulty that anything can be said of the substance thereof. For it is hard to speak of that which passes in the depths of the spirit if one have not deep spirituality; wherefore, having little thereof myself, I have delayed writing until now. But now . . . the Lord appears to have opened knowledge somewhat to me and given me some fervour (which must arise from your Honour's devout desire, for perhaps, as these words have been written for you, His Majesty desires them to be expounded for you).[5]

Here too is matter for reflection. John did not write, had nothing to say, except in the service of another. Through God's grace, he received what he said from those he wrote for. Teaching for him was a bilateral relationship in which he learnt from those whom he taught in the very act of teaching them.

When he was prior at Segovia (June 1588) Anne of Penalosa came to live there with one of her nieces who accompanied her to the convent when she visited John. It was at this period that John's brother, Francisco, came to visit him. John made a great fuss of him and spent a long time with him, remembering their mother who had died eleven years before.

Towards the end of his life, when he retired to Andalusia after refusing to be prior at Segovia, John first stayed for a while in Madrid. He sometimes visited Anne of Penalosa, who was staying with her brother, a priest. Then, following the orders he had been given, he said goodbye to his friends and retired to La Penuela.

But though the affections were important to John, it would be mistaken to suppose that they occupied the centre of his life. To chart this area of his life more fully, it would be necessary to untangle various strands in the network of his affective relationships. Affectivity is the realm where desire comes into its own. Affectivity is the expression of the unfolding of desire, and therefore a context for what is at issue in mysticism.

In order to avoid confusion it is wise to discuss first the false type of affectivity called passion, so as to be able to put it aside. In passion we see the unfolding of an imaginary world where desire represents the chance of complete satisfaction. In passion we find the belief that the true desiring relationship lies not in the bestowal of free gifts but in the filling of a want. Passion mistakes a means for an end.

But, having put passion aside, we still have two very different types of affection to deal with.

The first is love. In love we have the reciprocal gift of all that is me to all that is the other. But by receiving the other who has already received everything from me, I receive myself from the other. It is true that this copies the processes of passion. But instead of happening among the satisfactions of an imaginary world, this interchange takes place on the plane of reality, that is to say in frustration and sorrow, because what has been already given cannot be taken. It is exactly what we shall see in the interchange of beauties between the soul and Christ, where it is the true language of passion that is used, but not at all in a passionate sense. This interchange has a bearing on everything, even on the body—which is why the body is involved in the desiring relationship of love.

The second type of desire is friendship. In friendship the interchange of gifts is the same as it is in love—so that passionate friendship, like passionate love, is possible. But there is a basic difference—the interchange does not involve all that I am but only part of me, my freedom. I give my freedom to the other and I receive his from him while in the same process I give his to him and receive my own.

So the body plays a wholly different part here. In a sense it has no place at all. In love, desire seems to reach what it has as if and because it lacks it.[6] In love, the other's body, which is offered to me, appears as being painfully unpossessable, so I want to take possession of it by an act which marks both how near it is and yet how hard to grasp. Here is sexuality in the strict sense of the word. (And note that sexuality as such is the preserve of love, not of friendship; sexual love shows the whole gift of affection in a specific relation to the body).

In friendship, on the other hand, desire does not seek to own what it has not got as if it already owned it and because in a sense it does already own it. In friendship, the other's body belongs to me already insofar as it is possible for it to be mine. This certainly involves a sexual process, but only in that special sense that we call chastity.

To sum up: both love and friendship know that the loved

other is both given and out of reach at the same time. Love insists on the out–of–reach aspect, the difference between a couple, and therefore each makes claim to the other. Friendship is satisfied with what it has been given and therefore makes no claim to possession.

Various important conclusions can be drawn from this. The first is that friendship presupposes love. I cannot love in friendship if I do not also love in love. I cannot love in friendship if my body is not involved elsewhere in a relationship where it is desirable, where it is fully involved in desire. It is this relationship that leaves me free for friendship.

The second conclusion is that, in John's case, the love relationship was his relationship with God. This explains the use of sexual and nuptial imagery which is so transparent in his work. There is no doubt that some of his contemporaries were shocked by this, and it is probable that he would have been very averse to his writings coming before the Inquisition although he readily showed them to those who could understand them. And yet we are not dealing at all with an eroticism of mysticism, but rather with the distancing of eroticism. For God has no body and Christ's body is risen. The body is fully involved but in a relationship that does not involve sexuality in its literal sense. It is possible to see the Eucharist in an erotic sense, but to do so would be exactly the opposite of what is at issue here. What Jean–Jacques Rousseau said of Teresa of Avila—that her love was 'a love mistaken as to the beloved'—surely represents complete nonsense. Neither she nor John were ever mistaken about this.

So the relationship available to John for his brothers and sisters was one of friendship. This is the meaning of consecrated celibacy—it is love given in the context of God. The relationship of friendship is a powerful one, it can borrow the language of passion without any equivocation. Thus, when Anne of Penalosa asked John to pray for her brother about to celebrate his first mass, John could reply that he would certainly think of the brother, as he thought continually of the sister. Relationships of affection are alike in their references, their appeal, their distance from one another, their sheering off from one another, never halting—for then they would be trapped in gratifying the illusions of passion.[7]

Hence both John's freedom and his rigour with regard to

his friends. He met them, visited them, but he also parted from them, as at the end of his life when he quitted Madrid, or when he left Teresa so sad in Avila.

To his friends he was mainly a listener. He did not penetrate their lives, did not make their decisions for them, was respectful of their freedom. On the other hand his ear was close to them, close to what they were living through. He himself experienced the attention he gave them, as the passage from the prologue of the *Living Flame* shows. The events of their lives were lived wholly by them, not by him. But because they were lived wholly by them, they touched him as things touched him which he could not put into words. Perhaps what he wrote to Anne of Penalosa about the impossibility of speaking of what was in the *Living Flame* meant that much of it came from elsewhere. The events of their lives thus became events of his own life.

But this was only possible because his whole desire was centred in God. So it is important now to try to discover what it means to 'desire God'.

CHAPTER FOUR

I. To Desire God Provides a Meaning, but an Unexpected One

What do we mean by desire for God? Can the expression 'to desire God' mean anything to us now?

The question is crucial, having to do with whether God can be loved, and linked very closely to the assertion: God is not an object,[1] he is a Word that speaks to desire.

But where can I find this Word? In the Bible, in the sacraments, yes, but not at all as a word that speaks to me in the ordinary course of my life. I cannot see God, I cannot meet him, he is invisible. Even if Jesus Christ is God made visible, he has become invisible in his turn; he is risen, but no more accessible to us for that.

So God's Word has been spoken, still speaks, but is inaccessible—if I question God he will not answer me. Thus the believer who desires God with great love cannot turn towards an object, towards God as an object, towards a locatable person who would offer him a base. The believer, says John, is 'like to one that is suspended in the air and has no place whereon to find a foothold'.[2] So it would seem that desire for God cannot hope for fulfilment in God but is doomed to remain unconsummated.

Yet the paradox, as we know, is that beyond the *Ascent* and the *Dark Night* the great emptiness will be filled with the divine union. One of John's poems written independently of the four treatises describes this emptiness ('securely stay'd, yet without stay'[3]) but ends with man's transformation into pure love:

Since first I knew this love divine
Such wonders has it wrought in me
That naught but happiness I see

Alike if good or ill be mine,
For love transforms unfailingly.
The flame of heavenly love so sweet
I feel within me night and day,
Swiftly it whelms me with its heat;
Wholly am I consum'd away.[4]

That this transformation amounts to divinization, *The Spiritual Canticle* leaves no doubt. The soul is transformed in such a way that its life becomes God's life. The soul is described as 'divine and deified, so that in even its first movements it has naught whereto the will of God is opposed',[5] and this because 'the will of the soul that is converted into the will of God is then wholly the will of God'.[6]

It is within this framework that desire for God should be thought about, and with the only attitude to God that John really trusted, namely passivity, for guidance. From the whole storehouse of human resources, passivity (according to John) is the one attitude that puts us in the presence of God, for it hollows out the exact place where we may receive him. If we wonder what 'to desire God' means, then we must ask ourselves about 'passivity with regard to God'.

Passages defending passivity, and seeing it as the one infallible guide, abound in the *Ascent* and the *Dark Night*. Indeed nothing is easier than to summarize John's advice to beginners on the practical level: reject everything, and God too if he appears as a person, but do not reject what is received passively, like the 'substantial words',[7] 'for with respect to these words the soul should do nothing'; the same applies to certain feelings which the believer should just accept, for 'the understanding must do nothing in connection with these feelings, but conduct itself passively'.[8] In a word, John's advice to the believer who is afraid of the 'dark night' can be applied to all periods when there is emptiness of desire: do nothing:

If those souls to whom this comes to pass knew how to be quiet at this time, and troubled not about performing any kind of action, whether inward or outward, neither had any anxiety about doing anything, then they would delicately experience this inward refreshment in that ease and freedom from care.[9]

John's view of the pre–eminence of passivity can also be found by comparing the *Ascent* with the *Dark Night*. The *Dark Night* is intended for beginners who have already climbed the path of the *Ascent* and are in a more advanced state of perfection. But the *Dark Night* is more advanced than the *Ascent* only because of the passivity at work in it. In the *Dark Night* the 'dark night' is passive, whereas in the *Ascent* it is active. Yet the activity of the *Ascent* in fact consists of its being actively in a state of passivity.

Passivity aims at making the believer as supple as possible under God's action, at freeing him from any activity that might make him resist God's work upon him. The theme of the believer's flexibility before his Lord is to be found in the tradition of the prophets: seeing that Yahveh's thoughts were not man's thoughts, the believing community became recognized by its mobility, by its availability to God's will. 'Behold, like the clay in the potter's hand, so are you in my hand, O house of Israel'.[10]

But the image of the potter is far from being a conceptual one. It has practical reality, it is matter for meditation not for abstract thought. It does not have to be grasped by the mind but should be looked on as a piece of technical advice, it has to do with know–how not with knowledge. The significance of the suppleness and passivity suggested by the image of the potter should be looked at with great care, for to be like clay in a potter's hands is usually seen as a denial of man's freedom. But it is vital to show that this is not so.

The denial of man's freedom would have grave consequences for the question we are discussing. If God's full activity working on man were to deprive man of his freedom, then the power wielded by God would put God into competition with man's will. God's action would restrict another action. The encounter with man would become a battlefield, a struggle for the occupation of a territory—one part would be recognized as man's, the other as God's. The emptiness of desire would no longer exist. Thus the denial of man's freedom would make it impossible to think of God other than as an object.

But this is not all, for as this would–be desirable object has become active, it would in fact strike at the root of desire. God would be seen as a destructive and terrifying force; the

God of the universe would appear as a power that would certainly overwhelm us if only because of its superior strength. In other words, man's passivity before God would have obliterated him.

So we must try to see how passivity before God is not a blow at man's wholeness; that is to say, we must try to show that man's passivity before God is also man's freedom. Full freedom should be accorded to man in his relationship with God as illustrated by the image of the potter.

At first glance the situation does not seem favourable to our theory of God's action on us. The soul, when possessed by God, is destroyed, dismembered, thrown into confusion. It is aware of a sort of internal explosion which detaches it from itself and plunges it into unparalleled fear at the precariousness of its being. Its faculties are fragmented, separated from each other, so that the understanding does not know what the will wants, and the will is ignorant of what the understanding knows:

> From what we have said it may here be inferred how in these spiritual blessings, which are passively infused by God into the soul, the will may very well love even though the understanding understand not; and similarly the understanding may understand and the will love not.[11]

This is why passivity is at first experienced as suffering, anguish and threat, for passivity attacks the unity of the person, of the soul, for this is what is upset the moment suffering sets in. Consequently passivity at first presents itself as destruction. In passivity God is experienced as the pitiless force which destroys everything it encounters in the soul, to the point where it even produces the death of the soul itself. John goes so far as to say that if God did not provide for the soul by his grace, the soul would certainly die.[12] The reality of the idea of death in passivity cannot be pushed too far.

Yet it is from this position that we are able to take up our argument and recover what seems lost. John says that life is then maintained solely by grace. Yet it is difficult to distinguish between the grace that keeps man alive and God's action (hence grace again) by which man is fragmented and broken up—it is the same God, it is the same grace. So the Lord of the soul is revealed as bringing both life and death.

The death offered to the soul, that is to say the destruction of its active unity, is also its life. What is killed in the soul could well be its death, the dead part of it.

Now there does exist a death–bearing activity for the soul, the activity by which it claims that it gives itself its unity. This is not a benign operation, because if the soul believes that it can *give* itself a unity which in actual fact it *receives*, then it is deeply involved in a task by which it fetters its freedom.

The soul's claim to self-sufficiency can be understood in a paradox: our will is our own and at the same time foreign to us. In fact we cannot will at random because our will is our very selves, so that our deepest decisions arise from within ourselves. Of course we 'make' our decisions but nevertheless they are part of our being, they *are* our being. To take a look at our will darkly rising up in us allows us to put some space between us and ourselves so that we can look at ourselves and have the illusion that we are seeing not only what we will, but what we are. So real darkness is changed to apparent transparency. It is tempting here to claim for ourselves the directing of our own activity arising from our inner life. The soul is therefore able to believe that it *is* what it *sees* of itself. It is this ever–recurring narcissism that John calls activity.

So activity destroyed by the passivity of the mystical life is the process by which the soul assures itself imaginarily of the unity of its own life. So this activity is sight. Consequently the passivity by which the believer finds himself fragmented, by which he loses his unity, is the interruption not of an action but of sight.

John's texts confirm this interpretation. A passage from the *Dark Night* is significant:

> It is like the traveller, who, in order to go to new and unknown lands, takes new roads, unknown and untried, and journeys unguided by his past experience, but doubt-ingly and according to what others say. It is clear that such a man could not reach new countries, or add to his past experience, if he went not along new and unknown roads and abandoned those which were known to him. Exactly so, one who is learning further details concerning any office or art always proceeds in darkness, and receives no guid-

ance from his early knowledge, for if he left not that behind he would get no further nor make any progress; and in the same way, when the soul is making most progress, it is travelling in darkness, knowing naught. Wherefore, since God, as we have said, is the Master and Guide of this blind soul, it may well and truly rejoice, once it has learned to understand this, and say: 'In darkness and secure'.[13]

This passage is remarkable, first because it shows that here the role of passivity is played by blindness (the interruption of sight). God is the soul's guide and master because the soul is blind and because the type of blindness chosen to play the part of passivity is the type that discovers, invents, and explores new roads. The activity of the man who tries to direct the unity of his life is a limitation of his activity, and so another passivity. Whereas passivity with regard to God, inasmuch as it puts an end to the first type of activity, is the highest and fullest activity that can be imagined, the complete exercise of freedom. So passivity is the interruption of a certain type of activity, but with a view to liberating a power for action so great that it can only be compared to man's highest and most free activities—invention and discovery.

So it is along these lines that the problem of freedom can be solved—the problem of passivity and the potter's absolute sovereignty over his clay.

The activity which unfolds by means of passivity is an activity inherent in desire, the activity of desire itself, at least when desire is desire for God. Desire is active because it is a yearning, but passive because it is brought into being by what it yearns for. It cannot give an account of itself. It knows from deep within it that it is a gift. It actively reaches out to God at the same time as being passively received from God, so it learns that its autonomy is a gift, that it is given independence by the independence of God. God is the process that leads desire towards him. But the process that leads us towards each other because it brings the passivity that stops us looking at ourselves, the process that gives us independence through its independence from us—this is love. It is the very definition of love. Desire will go towards itself as to its goal. Yearning accepts itself as what it yearns for, so there is an indefinite increase of yearning which can only end up in infinity. Thus desire has access to an infinite increase of love, for—

> however great the agreement between it and the Beloved, the loving soul cannot fail to desire the recompense and the wages of its love, for the sake of which recompense it serves the Beloved; and otherwise its love would not be true; for the wages and recompense of love are naught else, nor can the soul desire aught else, than greater love, until it attains to perfection of love; for love confers no payment save of itself.[14]

Desire is a divine break in man, whose love for himself draws him towards God, as in loving God he loves too this break in his inner nature, which affects the whole of him. This immense break has no limits, for love in no way repairs this break but is more like an endless extension of it. This is divine certainly, as this blow to the depths of the heart draws man to his inner nature as towards God. Yet what he finds in this inner nature is not himself but the yearning for God. So this change to the divine in no way destroys the first of the demands made on him, for as a fulfilment it is still incomplete. But it does satisfy the opposite demand, as it is not barren, since it is wholly passive to the call of God.

So God is neither the aim nor the end of desire, but its beginning.

Such is the paradox of this break in man, by which desire is infinitely extended into its own nature. But in this case, the infinite is contained in desire, and so, by another paradox, desire extends within itself as it does outside itself, and its outwardness lies in its inwardness.

The logical conclusion of this should show us a man always buried in himself, always in ecstasy, lost to the world. But not at all. 'I do one thing only', said John, 'which is to love', though this was at a time when he was founding monasteries and reforming the order, a period of intense activity. The point is that his busy–ness did not distract him from the *one* thing he did, the magnet round which his other activities revolved. He thought only of God, but far from this preventing him from doing other things, it *enabled* him to do them. His actions became all the more significant as his love of God and hence his central will were projected onto each and every one of them. Never did everyday life take on more meaning than then; he was not a different man, he was the same man, but transformed.

The man of perfect love looks like other men, he cannot be recognized or singled out by any outward sign. It was one of Kierkegaard's best intuitions to point out how 'a knight of the faith' does nothing to help the ordinary man to see him as such, for, like the ordinary man, he goes home at night to eat his soup –

> and yet it is truly he. I draw a little nearer, I observe his smallest movements so as to try to catch him out doing something different, something of another kind, a little tele-graphic sign coming from the infinite, a glance, a look on his face, a gesture, a expression of melancholy, a smile, anything that might reveal the infinite as compared with the finite. But nothing! I scrutinise him from head to foot, trying to find some crack through which the infinite peeps— but nothing. Solidity everywhere. He observes Sunday. He goes to church. No glance heavenward, no sign of anything that makes him different from the rest of us, gives him away. If we did not know him, we would not notice him in the congregation, for his fine and powerful singing of the psalms merely proves that he has a sound chest.[15]

So the believer need not be described differently from the non–believer. The non–believer is not a believer minus some-thing any more than the believer is a non–believer plus some-thing. Yet it would be a mistake to think that faith does not show itself at all, even if the Word which keeps the believer in faith is hidden. After all, the activity of faith can be inves-tigated—it is produced in man when God's Word opens him to the passivity that alone allows him to accept it. This is an altogether human action, but it accepts the supernatural ac-tion by which God calls to it, and by doing so bring's God's action into being.

So through his Word God puts man at a distance, reveals transcendence to him and opens him to infinite love and desire for the One who has spoken. So man's openness to God produces a closing–in on himself, for transcendence is within him. The activity practised as passivity before God is no more 'conformable' with human nature than the other kind of activity. Absence of faith is not a lack. The believer's beliefs are not in competition with the non–believer's. He is the same man but has had a call from God, and by responding to it has come to love the incompleteness that the closing–in on himself reflects, for it is the sign of the loving Absolute's presence within him and outside him.

Belief in God—faith—is neither natural nor supernatural, it does not change man but strengthens him in his position. Faith reveals a poverty which is true riches, not the mere satisfaction of a crippled and unhappy man. Faith is freely-given bounty which seems more indispensable than the former sufficiency.

Atheistic thought about man sees him as sufficient–unto–himself, and in fact runs the risk of reducing him to inhumanity. Man has to have his Other, a Word by which he can identify himself. Only the Absolute Other gives him his full nature.

So 'to desire God' has a meaning. It is to desire because the Word has been given us. God is the origin of desire, but desire moves towards itself; it would disappear, however, it would never appear at all if it had to be content with this way of being. We cannot put desire for God in its proper place just by showing the distance between man and the Word that opens up the infinite and loving desire for God which, in its turn, divinizes man by giving him God and his separation from God. No, we must have real, concrete, ordinary actions if the relationship is to come to life.

Even so, these actions will not *express* as such man's relationship with God. Man does not act in charity in order to show his love for God, for this would be a betrayal of charity. How sad for our neighbour to be loved for God and not for himself! In charity, the believer acts not *for* God but *through* him. He does not do what he does because he loves God, but because God loves him. It is God's love for him, not his for God, that enables him to act in charity. So his actions are directed to those who receive them. But he is doing nothing in all this. He 'loves others' not 'for love of God' but for love of them, and through God's love for him. It is 'knowing' (but what does 'know' mean here?) that he is loved by God that enables the believer to have a genuine desire for reality—one that does not approach it with appetite, to devour it, but with the same infinite respect that God has for all his creatures.

Desire for God could not exist were there not also a reality for us to love. So it is important, after reviewing the events of John's life, to consider the world when seen in this light.

II. A Chronological Table of John's Active Life

John led a very full life and he travelled extensively. This chronological table of events portrays his activities in the clearest possible way.[1]

Date	Place	Offices, journeys, activities, works
1542	Fontiveros	
1548	Arevalo	
1551	Medina del Campo	Pupil first at the School of Doctrine, then with the Jesuits. Worked as sacristan in a church, as nurse in a hospital. Did weaving with his mother and his brother Francisco.
1563		Entered the Carmelite novitiate under the name of John of St Matthew. Made up pastoral songs in 'heroic couplets' (now lost).
1564	Salamanca	Student; discourse on contemplation (lost).
1567		Priest.
1568	Medina del Campo	Novice master.
Aug.		Foundation at Rio de Olmos (Valladolid).
Oct.	Duruelo	Constitution of the discalced Carmelites (?). Worked as a mason with a fellow friar and his brother Francisco, mostly at paving cells.
Nov.		Took the name of John of the Cross. Became sub–prior.

Date	Place	Offices, journeys, activities, works
1570		
June	Mancera (transferred from convent at Duruelo)	Novice–master.
Oct.	Pastrana	
Nov.	Mancera	Foundation at Alcala de Henares.
1571		
Jan.	Alcala de Henares	Rector of the college. Foundation of the convent of nuns at Alba de Tormes.
April		Travelled in New Castile.
1572	Pastrana	
April	Avila	Confessor and resident priest at the Incarnation.
1574		Visited the nuns at Medina del Campo
March		Foundation of the convent of nuns at Segovia.
1576		Captured by the 'calced' Carmelites but soon released.
Sept.		Meeting of the 'discalced' Carmelites at Almodóvar.
1577		
Dec.		Prisoner of the 'calced' Carmelites.
1578	Toledo	First draft of *The Spiritual Canticle*, the poems, and the poem of *The Dark Night*.
Aug.		Escaped from the prison of the 'calced' Carmelites.
Oct.		Chapter at Almodóvar. Excommunicated.
	Jaen (Monastery of Calvario)	Prior. Visited Beas—arranged altars, worked as mason laying floors of cells, weeded.
1579	Baeza	Foundation at Baeza, Granja de Santa Ana. Rector of the convent college. Worked on the decoration of the church and got the painter, Ubeda Juan de Vera, to do so too; the rector and professors of the university came to consult him. Regular visits to the sisters at Beas.

Date	*Place*	*Offices, journeys, activities, works*
1580		Gave the habit to a monk at La Penuela (Andalusia). Went to Caravaca (Murcia).
1581	Granada	
March		Chapter at Alcala de Henares, first chapter of the 'discalced' Carmelites as independent from the 'calced'. Elected third 'definidor' and prior of the convent of the Martyrs at Granada. The great treatises completed. The commentary of *The Spiritual Canticle* dedicated to Anne of Jesus, *The Living Flame of Love* to Anne of Penalosa. The *Cautions* written. Much humble menial work.
June		Travelled to Caravaca.
Oct.		Went to Castile. Meeting with Teresa at Avila.
1582		
Jan.		Foundation of the convent of nuns at Granada.
1583		
May		Chapter at Almodóvar.
1584		Manual work. Helped to build a cloister and an aqueduct with his brother Francisco, now aged over fifty.
1585		Elected second 'Definidor' and vicar–provincial of Andalusia resident at Granada.
Feb.		Foundation of the convent of nuns at Malaga.
May		Chapter at Lisbon.
Summer		Went to Malaga.
Oct.		Chapter at Pastrana.
1586		
May		Foundation of the Hermitage of San Roque (Cordova). Journey to Seville.
Aug.		Journey to Madrid.

Date	*Place*	*Offices, journeys, activities, works*
Oct.		Foundation of the monastery of monks at Cordova. Foundation of La Manchuela. Took part in the election of the prioress to succeed Anne of Jesus who had been transferred to Madrid.
Nov.		Journey to Malaga.
Dec.		Visit to the nuns' monastery at Caravaca. Foundation of the monastery of monks at Caravaca. Went to Beas.
1587		Went to Caravaca. Went to Beas.
April		Chapter at Valladolid. Prior of the Martyrs.
1588	Segovia	Chapter at Madrid; elected prior; general 'Definidor'; third counsellor of the Consulta. In the absence of Doria, presided for three months over the Consulta.
1591		General Chapter at Madrid; relieved of all his responsibilities. Returned to Segovia from Madrid to say goodbye to his friends.
Summer	La Penuela (Andalusia)	
Sept.	Ubeda	
Dec.		His death.

CHAPTER FIVE

I. The World and the Kingdom

References to the world appear several times in John's work. The most typical is certainly not the one at the beginning of the *Ascent*, where the world recedes and is set aside, but rather those that describe the re–emergence of the world as it comes back out of the shadows. There are two such passages.

The first comes at the end of the *Ascent* when, at the heart of man's denudation, creatures begin to show themselves. Here they are a source of joy in the renewal that comes after their loss. All created things awake in men the joy of God's existence.

It is worth observing that the re–emergence of the world should have come so quickly. John of the Cross was not a Francis of Assisi (though he was aware of him and loved him), yet neither had contempt for the world, while there is enough in John's work to show that he was a lover of nature.

The second reference occurs at the beginning of *The Spiritual Canticle* where the beauty of creatures speaks of an absent God, evoking his beauty with such intensity that the mystic wants to die of it.

The place of creation in John's work is thus a relatively modest one; the reality of the world is revealed to desire, not in its movement towards creatures but in its recoil in a process of wonder that reveals them. The world cannot be seen in its reality unless it is grasped in a quick glance that looks for something else and waits here only because it is frustrated of its true object. But since this frustration is a true element of desire, it is true to say that such a glance displays vivid attention to the reality of the world and its creatures. For creatures are not really seen and respected apart from this detached glance of wonder; it is when the believer looks at creatures while thinking only of God that he really sees them, and only then.

So the world does not receive very different treatment in the *Ascent* and in *The Spiritual Canticle*. In both it is the object of a respect expressed in one case by loss and in the other by recognition of its beauty. But the two themes are linked—loss brings out the beauty, while the sight of the beauty brings mortal loss.

However, the world appears a third time—as the field of action. As stated earlier, there has to be something real to love if God is to be truly desired. Desire for God demands action. But this action needs the support of something other than God to create a relationship with God. Action should be informed by desire for God while moving towards something other than God. Action should aim solely at its own world. It should 'forget' its origin, the better to reveal it.

We should take together these three ways the world appears: respect for the world, recoil in wonder at the world, and the chance really to act, to transform the world. The demands of the task are relatively easy to define—to initiate action while remaining wholly faithful to its meaning, so that it always embodies a *respect* for the real.

The main difficulty clearly is that action affects the fabric of existence where it is exercised. It has a tendency to destroy it. In order to act, I must modify reality. But this modification imposes on reality something foreign to it, though action would be falsified without it, it would be make–believe action, action that would not be achieved with the gravity proper to it.

So action should not simply introduce itself into reality to find its home there, it should change it to be accepted by it. Action cannot be satisfied by finding a ready–made place; it should create in reality its own potential conditions. Action has to be fruitful. Its birth and development have to bear fruit in reality.

Consequently, the analysis of action as embodiment of an idea is only partly sufficient as a way of thinking it. Action must respond to the reality it is ready to destroy and change. It must agree to what the reality is. This is what must be worked on if one wants to observe the demands just put forward. In this subtle decision on what Paul Ricoeur calls the assent to necessity[1] it is possible to imagine how respect for creation can be reconciled with real action. The stakes involve more than facile guesses and more than the scope of this book. Here at least perhaps are the elements of an answer to the irritating problem of the conflict between man and nature. To ask how action and reality are placed in relation to one another raises the question of culture and nature. Man has

—neither to struggle against nature as an adversary or enemy, as if he himself were not a biological being but wholly a product of culture;

—nor to follow nature and ask of it the key to its behaviour, nor to expect it to disclose what is natural and what is against nature.

Culture is

—neither mankind as such in its struggle against nature;

—nor what should follow nature as good in itself. Nature has no norm. It is hardly a guide, for everything, even the worst, is natural. If nature offered any sort of a norm it would certainly be that might is right.

Culture's task is to accept nature and transform it in this act of acceptance.

Here action has to agree to the effects it causes. It has to respect its own power to modify nature. By this means it discovers its own character. Along these lines lies the best hope of finding nature in the heart of action, loyal both to reality and its own transforming power. Reality, changed and so destroyed by action, re–emerges in action's power to modify it. This is what is needed to change reality while respecting it.

But what does this mean? For a *risk* is involved when reality passes into action. All action includes uncertainty. In face of that risk action has no assurance that it will be effective. To succeed I have neither to doubt nor to be confident that I shall be effective. Clearly if I doubt I shall fail to act. But if I am too confident of the effect of my action, reality will quickly correct me, since I shall not be flexible enough, nor grasp reality. For over–confidence drives me the other way, makes me think that the task is already done and so prevents my doing it—in my mind it is already done. At the start a plan of action never knows its full result. This gap between action and its fulfilment has its own irreducible necessity. It sets modest limits to all action which is obliged to humility through uncertainty of its success.

Action tests itself in face of this uncertainty, but the real test lies in achievement, for without that it would never take the risk. Action can only take the risk if even failure has some meaning, if it can *accept* failure. It has to go outside itself, to free itself in order to overcome uncertainty. It has to accept failure as a genuine risk. Failure must have a meaning for action to retain its full meaning even when it fails.

So it matters little whether I succeed or fail, for what I do already has a meaning, as this is not involved in failure or success. Though it is not a matter of indifference whether I succeed or fail, the issue is no more than *my* failure, *my* success, and things remain where they were. Action accepts this judgment on itself. It wants the world not only as it is, but as something more, a living wealth of possibilities able to limit its effort. The world seems wholly real only when action is ready to change it.

To accept risks assures action both of its effect and of respect. Again it has to rest on something other than achievements and results. Action requires conviction in its beginning no less than in its end. It has to appear well–founded.

At this point the question has shifted. For John, as for every believer, the world is not the final end of action, it is not the origin of a believer's actions, it is not *alone*. For not only is there the world, but there is also the Kingdom of God proclaimed by Jesus Christ. Two distinctions come before all others. The Kingdom is 'not of this world'[2] and at the same time it is 'at hand' among us.[3]

Taking these two assertions seriously leads to this: the Kingdom is *not* the world. It is not even *a* world. On the other hand the world is not the Kingdom. To be exact, the world and the Kingdom are wholly different in kind—they are not of the same nature. In fact they are so different as to have nothing in common. Yet they are not indifferent to one another. Just because they have nothing in common and wholly differ, they can pass from one to the other without mixing. Like glass and light, air and fire—to use John's favourite images—like night concealed in the heart of day—an excellent metaphor from Michel Henry[4]—their complete differences reflect a basic unity. The unity of the world and the Kingdom is complete, once this basic difference is taken into account.

Action would be well–founded if another world were placed beside this world, and outside it, where action could be initiated and established. But another world is not what the Kingdom means. There can be no question of a substitute–world. We must resign ourselves to foregoing another world, a world beyond, a world more real than this one, possible to live in or to aspire to.

The Kingdom is first of all what is not seen in the world. It has no part in it and remains in the centre of the visible world without belonging to it. So the world we see is nothing but a vision of this invisible Kingdom.

But the Kingdom is not merely a world where the meaning of the visible world is translated into unseen terms. It is clear where that would lead—to a visible world that has to be looked at with other glasses in order to see the unseen. So would come a vision of the world where the Kingdom would serve as its hidden side. Some passages in the gospels might lend themselves to this interpretation (the rich are the poor, the poor are the rich; the first shall be last; happy those who mourn; it was said of old—but I say to you). These texts are basic to what we have to say, but they cannot be taken so simply. For the Kingdom is not just a world set out before us, but *something else*. The Kingdom can only be visible to the world if it is itself arranged as a world. On the other hand it has neither effect nor meaning unless it is real. The point of interest is that the reality of the world depends on how it is presented. So it is important to define the relation between the invisible Kingdom and how the visible world is presented.

The Kingdom is not reached by the believer. It is not a place where he can be at rest. He can neither enter nor make his home there. He cannot conquer it—he can only conquer the world. It is not given to him to enter another world—on the contrary he is kept out of the Kingdom, for the believer remains in his own field of action, that is, the world. The Kingdom bring actions into being which cause the world to exist. The believer encounters the Kingdom when it sends him back to the old world, so that he can bring it into being by an action that the world itself is unable to initiate.

The Kingdom inspires actions, it is the basis of actions that are independent of the world. So one must not think that one can find the Kingdom by going beyond the external world. There is no other world—only this one.

But it is no use asserting this unless at the same time I mention the world's 'elsewhere'. As soon as I say 'only the world exists' I am led to contradict myself and add the implicit assertion 'the world has a meaning'. I would like very much to say that the meaning of the world is the world itself. But then—since meaning is nothing unless it is understood— this is to claim to know the meaning. This requires complete knowledge, and to claim that would be insupportable arrogance . . .

Without the Kingdom the world would be grotesquely split in two. On one side would be the contingent reflections of an individual, marked by his condition and the limits of his culture, and on the other an inconceivable reality enclosed on itself.

On the other hand to say that 'the world and the Kingdom exist' allows a true assertion of the world. This is not to say that the Kingdom does not exist, quite the contrary. The reality of one grows with the reality of the other. This life that seems so vain and these qualities we think so contingent assume their full weight. To paraphrase Malraux, who wrote that a life is worth nothing but nothing is worth a life, the world is worth nothing but nothing is worth the world.[5]

By means of the Kingdom our subjectivity is emptied but does not vanish. It no longer confines the meaning of the world to the limits of its culture. It becomes a subjectivity *foreign* to the world, for the foreigner is one who comes from elsewhere, who is born elsewhere, and for whom local habits are no more than habits.

So this foreign quality of the Kingdom leaves only the world to be seen. There is no other world than this, but things cannot be left here. Wholly unseen, the Kingdom turns back on itself and disappears buried in the bosom of the world. Only the world remains seen—it is sight *itself* and inclines to deny and efface any reference to the unseen. The Kingdom would then be on the way to establish the world in its full reality, but its strength is also its weakness, for the fact that it is foreign to sight conceals it from us. The Kingdom is always on the point of being forgotten, and once it is forgotten, there is an end to the reality of the world—it again turns back to itself and to its own meaning.

The Kingdom must not be forgotten. For the Kingdom to play its part in the world, we have to bring about the unseen division between the world and the Kingdom, to proclaim the difference between these two foreign entities.

Such is the believer's task.

The believer has to bear witness to his faith; a faith without witness would not reveal the Kingdom. If the Kingdom cannot be shown, as it is foreign to the world where everything is shown openly, it is *to be* shown. Otherwise visible reality would lose touch with it and would relapse into its pretense of solitude and its many illusions. So the believer must proclaim the Kingdom. He must say, 'the Kingdom *is*'. Once the believer says, 'the Kingdom is not of this world, but is among us', the world reverts to its full existence, for its own meaning is taken away from it. The world is then purified of this meaning, which is not to say that it no longer has a meaning, but that it has at last the meaning of its reality.

Here perhaps the essence remains to be grasped—how can the Kingdom be truly proclaimed? Out of respect for its foreign quality, any mere verbal assertion of the Kingdom has to be avoided. The Kingdom cannot be asserted in the same way as the world. One has to speak of revealing without showing or something of that sort. Otherwise, if the believer says, 'the Kingdom is a world—the true world', he is behaving like Jesus Christ's disciples when they had not yet understood that the Kingdom is not of this world. It was then that they asked him, 'Is it now that you are going to restore the kingdom of Israel'?[6] If it is foreign, the Kingdom must be shown to be foreign to any mere assertion, no less than to any theory. No theory can claim to be absolute.[7] Assertion of the Kingdom has also to involve some practical effect on the world. There must be a *production* of actions not initiated by the world. Precisely because actions are not initiated by the world, this production brings into being not two fields of action, but only one—the world itself. That is to say that the production does not depend on anything beyond (another world), but on a transcendence (what surpasses, and is not confined by, experience).

Action that reveals the Kingdom must show that it obeys

not the world but a Word that comes from elsewhere—if one can agree that a transcendence that is accepted *speaks*, or even that what unites us to the Other as such is a definition of the Word.[8] To welcome the Word and to accept its standards is to take account of the foreign quality on which its meaning is based. Already when I listen to somebody my inner silence gives attention to what is not myself, *who* is not myself. This is even more true when it is a matter of the Word of God. But this 'elsewhere' is not a message from beyond, it is not a question of listening to a Word given by God from a *place* outside the field of experience. The Word that he hears has always been given to the believer since it is in Scripture and in the community of belief that has already welcomed him. It is already there, coming from elsewhere, but wholly here.

To achieve his task the believer takes up this Word as addressed to himself. With this aim, acceptance of the Word undergoes the test of action that brings the Kingdom into being. So the believer plants the Word in himself. Really to listen is to pay attention in order to put into practice, so true it is that the Word is not received (whether this is the Word of God or anybody else) unless it changes the hearer in a way that makes action no longer the same. To put into practice is to listen truly to the Word. Not a practice that is deliberately applied, but one that is the authentic fruit of what has been received. That is to say that the Word is grasped for itself only to the extent that it restores the believer to the community, and in a vital way, so as to inspire actions—actions that bring the world into being. But henceforth they bring this about more completely, since the action that was based on the illusions of the world is eliminated from the world and situated in God.

There is only one action whose beginning cannot be defined, only one action that can be called free—to give more than one has, to strain towards what one is not with a boundless respect that rejects any weakening of the other's existence: to love.

If this is so, love is truly the presence of God among men, as it brings about the restoration of the Kingdom to the world, the presence of the Kingdom in the world. In the offer of love—which in this sense is called charity[9] as it brings the Kingdom into the world—the believer brings about the union of the world and the Kingdom. But this is how he openly displays the foreignness of the Kingdom and the world. He does not eliminate the foreignness, unless in himself.

Here we return to the matter of obedience. The believer is summoned to follow the example of his master Jesus Christ and to carry out not his own human will in the world but the basic will of the Kingdom, the will of the One who directs the world, the will of the Father. Here the believer shows a loyalty that is double and yet single.

So the will of God is not done by following definite demands that impose on the believer the conditions for his actions— these would be special directions coming from 'elsewhere'. The believer has not even to follow any instructions on what he should or should not do. The gospels are not a moral tract. On the contrary, the believer will be more given over to the will of God the more he works with wisdom and human reason. But neither is it for man simply to follow his human will—how in that case could be discover God's purposes? For the thoughts of God are not the thoughts of men.[10] It is the beginning of action (a beginning rooted in the Kingdom which is separated from the world yet co–extensive with it, separated from the world but with no other aim than to direct it to itself)—it is the beginning of action that uncovers a field of activity that is both wholly human and wholly obedient to God. I act as a believer when my actions are aimed at the existing world as the only reality at the same time as I refuse to be drawn away from the Kingdom and am attentive to God's Word with its power of inner renewal. My actions have to come not from me but from the One who can direct me towards reality. In this way I shall give myself up wholly to reality, yet remain wholly free in regard to it.

Now we must consider what allows the believer to declare his faith in this way, that is to say the ground on which his dual loyalty to the Kingdom and the world is disclosed—his body, since it is through this that he belongs to the world. In this sense the believer's body is the ground of the invisible, or, to quote St Paul, the temple of the Holy Spirit.[11] Also we have to consider the incarnation of man in his own body.

II. John of the Cross, Witness to the Kingdom

Faith proclaims the Kingdom. It has to show itself as the truth, that is to say, as what is here now and what is to come, as what is invisible yet can be seen, as present in a flash (like lightning that goes from one side of the sky to the other)[1] and at the same time hidden (if they tell you he is here, do not follow them).[2] The Kingdom is already among us, yet we are told to look for it in the future, to expect it. We have to wait for what has already been accomplished.

If the Kingdom is both 'among us' and 'not of this world', this does not mean that we have to look for another world, but to see this world as it really is. The Kingdom directs us towards the world, but discloses no more of itself.

The Kingdom has its own discretion and anonymity. It can be revealed only to those who have already seen it, can be displayed only in its own truth. Otherwise it vanishes. It shows itself only in a certain way of looking at this world, and nothing is more foreign to its genius than to be seen for its own sake. In this sense it eludes the category of the sacred, it does not operate by dividing the sacred from the profane, but by making the sacred so universal that it becomes the norm and form of the profane. No longer a chosen people but salvation for all, no longer priests and kings but a royal priesthood for all who are baptized, no longer sacred places set apart but a God everywhere adored 'in spirit and in truth', so that there is no longer any distinction between Samaritans and Jews, no longer a division of time between the Lord's Day and profane days, but acknowledgement that the sabbath is made for man, not man for the sabbath.[3] The Kingdom is not a ground to reach, but the heart of a world of another kind (which is not another world).

If the Kingdom can only be proclaimed by casting a certain light on the existing world, it becomes impossible to show it without living it. A certain way of life proclaims it. Here the idea of witness arises. To be a witness is to relate what one has seen. What has one seen? One never bears witness as one intends. Witness cannot be directed and manipulated. It is a basic witness of what surpasses me, beyond anything I think I believe. To be a witness is to present the truth of a reality observed through myself. I prove the reality I witness by my own reality. In this way I can give to others something that does not belong to me. To be a witness is to offer oneself, with all the risks and dangers this involves, not as a proof of what one witnesses, but as the impregnable ground of what one lives by.

But then it becomes impossible to state what one has witnessed without precisely disclosing its strength and its secret. There is a whole dimension of personal, hidden and impenetrable intimacy whose significance has already been discussed in dealing with spiritual direction. Witness can only be given by bringing together oneself and what can hardly be related without some risk to modesty: *witness is wholly identical with oneself.*

As one would expect, this discretion can be found very particularly in John—never the least glimpse of autobiography, never the least interest in what happens to him. He accepted the greatest responsibilities, threw himself into the boldest and most perilous actions in the same way and with the same firmness that he accepted the checks that were at times imposed on him. His whole being is hidden, but not by any lack of spontaneity or preference for secrecy. We have seen that he hardly made any mystery of himself, and his candour is proverbial. We cannot unseal this secret.

Yet his contemporaries were not deprived of it. Many marvels and miracles were told of him. But we read of them with some embarrassment. They are the usual baggage of all the 'lives of saints'. It seems a waste of time and effort to try to sort out what is true and what is false. There are two attitudes to this question, both equally unsatisfactory.

On the one hand we can take the facts at their face value. After all, nothing is impossible with God. But then we drop into a literary form that has always seemed to us singularly trivial, one that turns its back deliberately on what to us is the essence of faith—the heart of acceptance in face of which nothing subsists. Accounts of ecstasy leave us cold and seem to take us away from naked faith, so praised by John, into a grotesque disregard of what really matters.

On the other hand we can try to play down the abnormal happenings, to show that there is no conflict between them and those of nature, the better to show God's greatness through this veil of reality that is the sovereign gift made to us. But here too disillusion awaits. For there is no doubt that those who have experienced these things have known something much deeper than treatment of this kind would admit. And if they could not record it differently, how are we to believe that we could relate it better? By what right and by what strange lack of respect should we take it upon ourselves to eliminate the mythical and the mystical?

When John was quite small, he fell into a stretch of water; a wonderfully beautiful Lady held out a hand to draw him out, but he was afraid of soiling it so refused her help, finally being rescued by a peasant with a long pole.

During a journey between Arévalo and Medina del Campo, a grotesque creature issued from a marsh and tried to hurl itself on John and gobble him up. But John made the sign of the cross and the creature went back into the water.

When he was at the School of Doctrine John fell into a well from which he emerged safe and sound—the Virgin had raised him up. Everybody saw this miracle. It came to the ears of the hospital adminstrator who summoned John to visit him. This was how they met.

At the convent of the Incarnation a nun, Maria de Yeres, died unconfessed. But John raised her up again and gave her the last sacraments. She could then die in peace.

There is no end to the number of nuns possessed by the devil and effectively exorcized by him.

In June 1588 the monks noticed that a very splendid pigeon had followed John from Granada to Segovia. This splendid pigeon neither cooed nor ate with the others.

What are we to say of all this? Nothing, beyond the fact that doubtless many things got mixed up, and that we cannot put possession by the devil and the whims of a pigeon on the same plane. But in John's writings there is no warrant for anything but a deliberate refusal to consider these incidents. And as for his personal reaction, when we can discover it— always related by a third person—it shows the greatest reticence. John Evangelista, his favourite companion, who had asked and been allowed to be always in the same monastery, so devoted was he to him, had heard John relate the incident of the well at Medina del Campo—it was a useful plank that saved him and not at all the Mother of God. As for the pigeon, John quietly ordered the excited monks to pay no attention to it.

At Baeza there was an unusual atmosphere of piety. The monks confessed daily. But there were also many 'devout women', possessed and ecstatic. John gave up some of his energy and humour to exposing them. There was one who, pretending to be in ecstasy, was brought out of it by John in an exemplary way. A tumbler of water was to be poured over her head to bring her to a more reasonable frame of mind. But the glass broke at the last moment so that glass and contents were dropped—but the 'devout woman' moved aside to avoid them, proving that she was in less of an ecstasy than she thought.

At Lisbon there lived a nun who bore the stigmata and worked miracles. Levitation was her peculiar gift. All the chapter went to see her except John who obstinately refused despite pressure brought on him.

This indifference to miracles and marvels makes very good sense. At bottom, the nature of these phenomena hardly matters. They are of no interest to faith nor could they be. Perhaps they have some value as signs to those who experience them— but it is better not to talk about them, for they would like to dispense with the act of faith which is irreplaceable and carries much more weight than the greatest miracle.

So we must return to John's very grave discretion. His life was fully human and wholly fulfilled.

His education was that of a gifted student. It began at the School of Doctrine at Medina del Campo. Children were taught crafts suited to their abilities. John tried several but, despite his good will, did not really succeed with any. Yet he retained a taste for painting and sculpture. Some of his drawings were remarkable, in particular one of the crucifixion seen from above in the extraordinary perspective copied by Salvador Dali. He was still more gifted in literary pursuits.

After his School of Doctrine, he went to the hospital in Medina del Campo. There he was day–orderly and almoner. He also went to the Jesuit college where he studied well between the ages of seventeen and twenty–one. He became a good Latin scholar, working at night when his hospital duties allowed it. The patients thought highly of him. The head of the hospital took an interest in him and wanted to make him the chaplain.

All this shows nothing out of the way. With no trouble, no sensational conversion, no setbacks, John became a priest. He only hesitated when it came to the choice of an order. He was a novice with the Carmelites, but wanted to be a Carthusian. It was Teresa's demand for reform that decided him to stay with the Carmelites. But that did not mean that he allowed himself to be carried away by events. He eagerly accepted Teresa's offer to take part in the reform, but imposed one condition—that he would not have to wait too long for this to begin.

Next came his stay in Salamanca as a student. The university of Salamanca was the most famous in Spain and one of the most respected in Europe. As a Carmelite he received a dual education, in the university itself and in the Carmelite college of San Andrés. Students were obliged to follow both courses, given exclusively in Latin. A fine was imposed on teachers who used the vernacular. Yet among students and professors a movement was beginning in favour of Spanish. It is not known how this debate affected John of St Matthew. He always wrote in Spanish, though the form of the phrases in his commentaries bears a striking resemblance to Latin constructions.

John was an excellent student as far as is known. This is proved by his being made 'prefect of studies', a post reserved for the best students. We also know that his life at this period had an influence that extended even as far as Medina del Campo.

On the other hand we know little about who taught him. Perhaps, as the dates tally, he studied under the mystic Fray Luis de Leon who was investigated in 1572 by the Inquisition for having translated *The Song of Songs* into the vernacular. However the content of the teaching in theology and philosophy that he received shows in his works—scholasticism. The great teaching of Thomas Aquinas in the thirteenth century had renewed philosophy and theology from top to bottom by integrating the two disciplines in line with Aristotle, at a time when Christian universities in Europe were more inclined to Plato. By the sixteenth century scholasticism had triumphed, but perhaps no longer had the zest and savour

that had marked it three centuries earlier. Yet it offered one
of the boldest and most complete systems of thought that
have ever been, even if it was a cumbersome apparatus for
treating refined ideas. John took up the terms of this already
established teaching. He brought nothing new to it but made
use of it for what he had to say. His original thought used it
as a tool but without modifying it. His university education
was nothing out of the way for a successful student in sixteenth–century Spain.

Where, then, are we to find John's witness? In the Carmelite reform?—but that was Teresa's work, and although he
responded to her call he brought nothing new to it. He introduced no reform in doctrinal teaching. There is no precise St
John plan of reform, even though this dominated his activity
and he was the author of the constitution for the 'discalced'
Carmelites of Duruelo.

His real witness was based on his gift for contemplation.
With him contemplation was the action of actions, whatsoever
form it took, visions or none, ecstasies or none, delectation or
aridity. But this action was enclosed on itself and revealed
nothing but excellent poems and commentaries on them.

Apart from this central activity his second witness lay in
teaching. This is certainly what members of religious orders
valued most in him. It is said that at Beas the nuns stopped
everything so as to come and listen to him. What had he to
say? All that he wrote and spoke developed out of his contemplation. He talked neither of himself nor his listeners. He
spoke only of what really matters, what they knew already—
Jesus Christ. It was a statement at a depth beyond all other.
All one can say of his teaching—apart from its message—is
simply its worth as witness; it aroused the sense of their own
life in those who heard, and revealed the ground of prayer.
'Much given to work, prayer and the monastic cell'—that is
how Teresa summed him up after her interview with him in
1567. That is why he satisfied her so deeply and she considered him the best confessor that had ever come her way.
It is always shattering to learn one's own peculiar truth from
somebody who appears not to know nor to want to know. He
directed everyone to their desire for the Absolute, the Absolute revealed, crucified and arisen.

So we are brought back to reading his works. His witness

as a contemplative and a teacher can be grasped only in his character, and this is hidden from us. A few accounts give us a glimpse of his humour,[4] the extent of his influence,[5] his inner freedom,[6] and his understanding of others.[7] But characters have the formidable privilege of being *inconceivable*. The more we love someone, the more quickly we forget the sound of his voice, the look of his face, and even the way he walks, when he is away. Hardly have I left the one I love than I need to see him again, for only he can reveal himself. Yet this blank means nothing, for I know that I shall recognize him at a glance, just in the shock of the difference between him and the memory of him.

So to discover the 'real' John is an effort in vain. Yet there remains one recourse. Parado. ical though it may seem, the secret of our individual character is in our body. So the final attempt to find John through his writings requires an investigation into the place of the body in the balance of his thought, and a review of this in the perspective of his own body.

CHAPTER SIX

I. The Body

In carefully reading John of the Cross, one finds that a subject usually treated with reserve, the body, is a necessary element in his way of thinking. It occurs rarely in the stages of the mystical journey, at least on the surface, and even when it is openly mentioned, the references are so scattered that it is hard to bring them together. Also when it emerges from the shadows and is in fact mentioned, it cannot be set out in the form of definite teaching, such as John gives on appetite, or desire, or spiritual direction; and even when brought together, the references to the body fail to tell us much, as their meaning comes less from them than from the relation they bear to the whole journey.

One can quote a few texts where the body is shown to be affected by the mystical life, when the mystical life reaches such intensity as to produce a shock so violent that it shakes the body:

> And these are sometimes suddenly caused in the soul by its mere recollection of certain things—sometimes of very small things. And they are so readily perceived that at times they cause not only the soul, but also the body, to tremble.[1]

So at the climax of the divine union the soul undergoes emotions of overwhelming delight that have at their centre a 'poisoned arrow' which increases love so that the body is wounded 'as came to pass when the seraph wounded the soul of St Francis [of Assisi] with love inflicting upon him five wounds [of Christ crucified] . . . and he was actually wounded in his body'.[2]

The body is also mentioned in *The Spiritual Canticle* and

given a somewhat different meaning. The soul, intoxicated with the Beloved, thinks that it must escape from the flesh, but is recalled to its true home, the body. Certainly the flesh is one of the three enemies of the soul, the two others being the world and the devil.[3] But the flesh—which partly at least involves the body—receives the same treatment as the world. It is not the qualities of the body or of creatures that turn them into enemies of the soul, but their use in a way for which the soul bears responsibility. To shun the body is one such abuse. The body is not to be shunned except at the cost of an illusion. On the contrary, the soul has in fact to exist in the body for it is there that Christ awaits it.

From this arises the dialogue between the soul and the Beloved: 'Withdraw them, Beloved', says the soul. 'Return thou, dove', replies Christ. On this John comments:

Withdraw them, Beloved!
That is to say: Withdraw these Thy Divine eyes, for they make me to soar aloft, issuing forth from myself in highest contemplation above that which my physical nature can bear. This she says because it seemed to her that her soul was flying out of her body, which is what she desired: for this reason she begged Him to withdraw His eyes—that is to communicate them to her no longer in the flesh since in this wise she could neither bear them nor enjoy them as she would desire, but to communicate them to her in the flight which she was about to make from out of the flesh. But this desire and flight the Spouse prevented, saying:
Return, dove,
for the communication which thou art now receiving from Me belongs not yet to that estate of glory to which thou now aspirest. But return thou to Me, for it is I Whom thou seekest, wounded as thou art by love. And I also, Who am like to the hart wounded by thy love, now begin to reveal Myself to thee in thy lofty contemplation, and take recreation and refreshment in the love of thy contemplation.[4]

Until it has crossed the threshold of death, it is in the body that the soul has to love and be loved.

These quotations have a great value, but they do not tell us enough. Judging from them, we could not even say that for John the purpose of the body is simply to remind man of his bodily and fleshly state. We have also to take into account a number of other texts whose teaching would be quite different, but where, unfortunately, the body is no more than mentioned.

This reserve that John maintains about the body is easily understood. The body is bound up with the senses, perception, the world; now for the mystic God is his centre of gravity or, to be more exact, God taking hold of the believer in faith. From this point of view the body has to be somewhat set aside because it has not the taste of God. *Nothing* has the taste of God. God has no taste, no flavour. This is one of the first things the believer learns when he listens to John—to choose the unpleasing rather than the delectable,[5]

> For to seek oneself in God is to seek the favours and refreshments of God; but to seek God in oneself is not only to desire to be without both of these for God's sake, but to incline oneself to choose, for Christ's sake, all that is most distasteful, whether as to God or as to the world; and this is love of God.[6]

In essential matters the body is set aside, as being neither an enemy nor a friend. Yet this dismissal of the body does not end the matter. Although the body as such gets no special mention, most of the questions in John's work assume the body in their treatment. This is the case with desire, for desire without a body can only be imagined by weakening its power. The same is true of the world. If the world exists for us, if the believer is in the world, it is because he has a body.

On this point the subject of love seems to us even more decisive. Qualities in the love of God for the soul and of the soul for God forbid us to consider this as a platonic and disembodied love. On the contrary, it belongs very much to the body. John's idea of love assumes a union of persons who still remain distinct at the heart of it. It assumes that the Beloved rejoices in the beauty of the soul and that the soul rejoices in the beauty of the Beloved, as they give this beauty to one another:

> And I shall see myself in Thee in Thy beauty; and Thou wilt see Thyself in me in Thy beauty; and thus I may be like to Thee in Thy beauty and Thou mayest be like to me

in Thy beauty, and my beauty may be Thy beauty, and Thy beauty my beauty; and thus I shall be Thou in Thy beauty and Thou wilt be I in Thy beauty.[7]

It is easy to see that this quotation describes the *passion* of love—surprising but indisputable. Perhaps it is this freedom of John's, suspicious of moral good[8] but celebrating passionate love between the soul and God, that makes him so attractive to us.

Of course this is a metaphor. It is certain that human expressions in John's writings are metaphorical, and that although the description of human love and God's love are made in the same terms—those of married love—there is a distance between man's love for woman and God's love for the soul. In fact if the same terms are used, it is precisely because the realities described are *different* from one another.

We have to note this difference and also that the distance between man's love and God's love is the same as that which separates God from man who, in fulfilling himself, has the opportunity to live the life of God on this earth. Human love and God's love can be described in the same terms, not because they are one and the same reality, not because there is just a difference of degree in the two forms of love, but because human love and God's love stand in a relation that can only be conceived as analogical—a remote image of the same relation. This analogy forbids any thought of God's love as a disembodied version of human love. On the contrary, the reality of human love and its use of the body seems to be a metaphor, a remote and weaker image of God's love. It is human love which is a metaphor of God's love, not the other way round. If the body serves human love, *a fortiori* it serves God's love, in a wholly different way that does away with any erotic element but not with its bodily aspect.

But John's reflections on the body are not confined to the context of love. Suffering and sacrifice are also involved in the journey, they too have to be related to the body. Disembodied suffering is no less hard to imagine than disembodied desire. It is important too that Christ's passion, where God in fact has pledged the Body of the Son, is the archetype of suffering and sacrifice. Suffering and sacrifice that failed to involve the body would not make sense.

Finally there is death, which often appears to the believer either as the end, wanted but never granted at the heart of the mystical journey, or as what already happens in some sense during the journey, in a different way from the change of a body into a corpse. It would be too easy to say that this is 'another death', a death not involving the body, for why then call it death? And why should Christ, whose way has to be imitated, have chosen this path and gone to a real death, death on a cross?

So the body is bound up with every stage of the mystical journey.

We have then to ask who is the subject of the mystical journey? Is it man, as union of body and spirit? Is it the believer's soul, taken in contrast to the rest of his being? Is it the being of flesh and matter? Here there can be no dispute, the question can be answered at once, for John is quite clear on this point: it is the 'soul' that embarks on the mystical journey—this strange part of man, peculiar to the Christian tradition, which is neither 'spirit' nor exactly the Jewish 'heart' (where body and spirit are indissolubly united), but more or less defined by 'man on his way to salvation'.

But what is this aspect of man? It is not clear that it excludes the body, since the resurrection of the body is part of the Creed.

On the other hand the word 'soul' in Christian teaching does not always have the meaning here assigned to it. Often it has taken its meaning in opposition to the body. Must then the relation of soul to body be discussed?

That would be a false trail, for to John the soul plays a part very close to the Jewish 'heart'. It is the soul that desires, that lives in the world, that loves, suffers and dies, and thus—through the themes treated in the four treatises—behaves *also* like a body. The body in the sense of flesh, external, a mere envelope, in short as opposed to the soul, occurs only briefly and always in a way much less important than the body summoned to take part in Life and Resurrection, the body which seems to John to be part of the soul itself, as a phase in its existence.

So the question of the relationship between body and soul may be dismissed, for with John it is the soul that matters even when it is the body that matters. The real question is the bodily nature of the soul, the process of salvation as it concerns the body, the whole process of incarnation.

The process of incarnation, of course, is what sends man from the Kingdom into the world. The believer is taken and set in the world as the world is set before the believer. He cannot make his home in the Kingdom, for it is the Kingdom that sends him into the world. And what inserts the believer into the world is his body.

We speak of a process because it is a sending–out, but this is no more than a metaphor. The process of incarnation sets man in his body, but there is no time factor in this. Incarnation is always already achieved, it is a result, the process of being sent is never disclosed till after it has happened. The proof of this is that only the believer, when he accepts the faith, understands what his position is.

That is to say that the body is above all a place. The relationship of the body to the believer is first and foremost a topological reality, as a sign of where the incarnation takes place. It is the place where the believer has always been sent into the world.

This last point is not without effect, for it shows that the body cannot be viewed as a prison. The body is not an envelope, a prison for the soul. Indeed this view of the body— as a fleshly deposit that will one day be 'cast off'—is a platonic concept and at the opposite pole from Christianity. If the body is a prison, then we can only imagine that the soul would be elsewhere. But for the Christian (as opposed to the platonist who would provide a special place for the soul outside the body) there is no such elsewhere. To put it more clearly, the Kingdom—the only 'elsewhere' that could be considered—is not on high, but here among us, and this is what sends the soul into the body and gives the soul a home in the body.

At this point it is worth noting that man's origin cannot lie in an elsewhere that exists of itself. If it could, the body would be a prison for the soul that wants to 'return' to the Father. But the body has always been there. It had no life in the elsewhere of the Kingdom[9] before being called into existence. The summons to exist and presence in the world are simultaneous, so that body and soul are summoned together. That is to say that man's body is created and not brought into

being, insofar as it has an outward appearance elsewhere than
in its beginning; it is not born in the very centre of its origin
in the way that allows the Son, the one and only Son, to
express the sum of the Father. The human son is never an
only son, for even if he is the only son of his father, he remains
the child of a family, issuing from a repeated series; he does
not express his father, he is in no sense the Word of his
human father, any more than he is the Word of God the
Father. Here again the metaphor is to be interpreted the
other way round—it is the Son who is the only son, for human
sons are always some among others in a repeated series,
because they have no beginning that subsists of itself, no
Father, unless by adoption.

Incarnation then is not a bringing into being in an elsewhere that is expressed or defined or revealed, but a process
already brought about and to be repeated till the end of time.
In this way the body appears, in the world's network of
definite elements, as a *sign* of incarnation, of the constantly-
achieved process that goes from the Kingdom to the world.
But the sign might suggest an emptiness of some sort. It is
nothing of the kind, for the sign of incarnation is a body, a
sign of fullness. My body is not a gap in the fabric of reality,
but one of the elements of reality, a true and constituent part
of it, a complete element among complete elements. We have
then to reject any idea of incarnation which would display it
as a grace filling a bodily container of animal consistency, or
as an imprint etched on the flesh as the negative sign of a
process aimed at upsetting the order of the world. Such an
image would endow the realities of the Kingdom and the
world with the same nature, making them merely different.
That would destroy the basic foreign element that allows both
to pass into one another.[10]

The fact that the body is complete, not empty, entails a
second consequence that is basic, and this brings us closer to
another truth about the body. It is, as already said, the place
where incarnation happens. That this place is full and not
hollow leads us to add that the body is not unseen but seen.
The process of incarnation is unseen, but the body reveals
that what is unseen can be seen. That is why it appears as a
result always already achieved, never a process in the course
of development. The body is what is seen of the unseen drive

into the world, not as a lack or an emptiness, but as the filling of an emptiness never recognized before.

It is not enough to say that the body is seen, it is *wholly* seen. It is visibility itself. It is visible; it is what is seen of the unseen. In the enthusiasm of this assertion, it is tempting to say that it is seen through and through. But that is not true. If the body is seen, it is given over, offered, it has its own consistency, its own fate, always before, behind or beside another object, taking a full part in objective reality. Consequently it would be better to say that the body is visible and therefore opaque. The body can always be opened and dissected like any other thing; everything in it can be ceaselessly examined, brought to light, described and commented on without anything else but what is visible appearing. But what is seen hides an infinite number of other elements, which can also be seen.

Wholly given over and uncovered, it can be seen day and night, but it is also enclosed on itself, opaque. It is spread out without ever really disclosing those depths and differences in levels of reality, those distinctions in states of being that all life sets before us—not even the possible and the actual, the unreal and the real. There is no more than a solid body, a solidity in which the physiological apparatus tirelessly operates. It is this thickness that protects the organisms of the body with their distinctive elements superimposed on one another. Even in the best integrated circuits of the nerves—to understand which requires the elaboration of levels of being—the body remains material, that is to say exposed, from rib to rib, unavoidably and for ever, or at least until death.

This condition of the seen being also the opaque and consequently the separate, the discontinuous, the stretched–out characteristic of the organic, brings about the vulnerability of the body (and this is the fresh image in which it now appears to us).

It would be wrong to think that the body is fully at home in the reality of nature, sunk in a network of definite elements interbound with one another. It would be wrong to think this although the body is *also* attached to the world in this way. But it must be noted that the body's organic thickness is threatened by its insertion into the world, for all the dangers that the body faces come to it from the world. It is there, exposed in both senses of the word (that is, displayed and open to risk), and the more it shelters in the protective bosom of nature, the more chance it has of a blow that could interrupt and destroy the patient, obstinate working of its machinery. The body lives in itself and in the world, but danger lives there too; to be at home in the world means to the body not only life but the risk of destruction.

Certainly Deleuse and Guattari are right when they begin their *Anti-Oedipe* by saying that the body, as a working model of desire, 'works all over, sometimes without stopping, sometimes at intervals. It breathes, it heats, it eats'.[11] It is true, the body works. But above all it is vulnerable, it can break, it *will* break. Now this risk of vulnerability shakes the firmness and solidity of the organism. The vulnerable body is not only this exposed display of reactions that, at the slightest hint, carry out their work in the service of an organism so vast that it could spread without difficulty to the dimensions of the universe. No, the body's fragility and vulnerability shake it to its depths, uncover in it a depth of being and a chance of independence from what threatens it and destroys it. In short, its vulnerability brings to it that depth of being which it would otherwise lack. Indeed the chance of destruction adds depth to the body, for it makes it see and be seen, and so through its vulnerability it reaches its own visible truth. This visible truth becomes aware of itself in its vulnerability, where the body achieves independence on its own basis, withdrawn from the world and things. Only what is vulnerable is seen, watched, discerned, threatened, raised above its attachment to the world and exposed to danger. Raised above the network of its connections with the world, vulnerability is seen and offers itself as visible truth.

In this not only is the body visible to itself, but its completion is no longer just a completion but a visible completion, and with that the world becomes visible and seen. With vulnerability the visibility of the world is itself attracted and takes on a meaning for me through my body. If it is true that to discern involves my seeing the meaning of things, this meaning only shows by its connection with my true interest, that is to say the problem of life and death, of what as a body I am.

Vulnerability makes things visible against a background of the threat of death. Death can strike the body which watches and questions things, but it can also strike complete and visible things and beings in their fragility. Beings are only seen against a background of the absence of being, which brings them forward and forces them to be seen. Then every being is detached from the sum of nature, everything in the world can be a threat or threatened when the body turns to them. What is seen is displayed against a background that is quickly hidden—a flash that comes from the chance that being may annihilate the forces opposed to it. Vulnerability is always present in the heart of appearances. As for the body, so for the world, there is an abyss that allows a real being to be something other than a being yet still visible.

So we come to a new definition, a new truth about the body. It is a way of getting at man's vulnerability. By the body man becomes vulnerable. Man's vulnerability is only true insofar as he has a body, for death is not only the death of the body, it is also the death of man—which clearly does not necessarily imply his destruction. That man has to pass through death means that he has a bodily form, much more than that his body dies. Man does not undergo death without all his being undergoing it too. What is struck by this event is called the body. Man's vulnerability is the sign of his being driven into the world. So the body is not man's truth, only his mortal centre.

Taken in this way, seen as the vulnerable centre of man, the body stands for passivity, for this is the result of being given over to existence. We could say that the body is itself man's passivity. Now if man is passive through his body, if all his passivity works through his body insofar as his body is the way to reach that supreme passivity which is vulnerability, then the mystic who relates himself to God through passivity, who sees himself as above all passive, who gives an absolute value to passivity over action—then the mystic must see the body as pre–eminently important. The mystic is above all his body.

But the body has an activity, that of its organs. Its vulnerability is the vulnerability of an activity. In the same way its passivity can only be grasped as the passivity of an activity always under threat.

Vulnerability now shows itself as a chance, but it is not only a chance, it is also a fate. The mortal end of the body—and so of man—is a fate. This brings us to another point. The process that carries the incarnate truth of the body through its visibility, its vulnerability and its passivity, begins to deviate. The body's truth, the fact that it is threatened, fatal and vulnerable, begins to seem like a *respite*. It appears as what can be destroyed *and* as what will be destroyed. Its future death, unknown to the living being, affects the whole course of daily life, enters into it and changes it in depth. The soul's passivity is shown by the mortal nature of the body whose activity is interrupted and which in the same way finds its truth only in the respite granted to it. So the body as such takes on a new shape. Vulnerable, passive and visible, it is most of all what has not yet been reached. Consequently, and this is the main point, it does not possess but waits for its truth, though this when it comes will destroy it as a body. So it is sustained in its truth away from its truth. There is no truth for the body, or rather its truth is to be away from its truth.

Because of the respite granted to it and which is its own existence, the body then becomes the place of living and waiting. It is aware of the basically equal interchange between pleasure and pain. Life for the body is this foresight into vulnerability, the practice of vulnerability and passivity, the refusal of passivity that brings the triumph of activity, yet this itself discloses how brief is the respite granted to it. The respite is a period of enjoyment and disillusion—and pain. The body is the seat of pleasure, not through any quality of its nature, but because the pain that it awaits does not always come. In the same way the body experiences pain because the pleasure of living and working normally is not always granted but is brought back to its destined truth by frustration and destruction.

Pleasure and pain alternate. Both disclose their nature by means of the time they occupy. They are the respite, the occupation of time, and they are satisfied in being at home. At home in time, both pleasure and pain disclose the ability to endure—they are basically what can be endured. What pleasure offers (though it is always disillusioned) is the vision of being at home in a reasonable and invulnerable body, saved without undergoing death, a life fulfilled in itself as it swallows up everything in the conditions of an apparatus put to the satisfaction of desire. Similarly what pain gives is the chance of enduring in spite of everything, through force of character and soul—the chance of being at home with pain.

But both only show what can be endured because they are remote from their truth. Pleasure is no more than a moment, in other words it fails to be really at home in time. And pain, nearer the truth because, despite everything, it endures to the limit of what is bearable, goes back to something deeper than itself that is not met so long as pain as such is present. Yet pain belongs to and is rooted in the body, truly incarnate in time, and time (in the context of pain) no longer passes but stops, changing a moment into a duration that goes on and on.

This development discloses the truth of the body, close to the truth where it endures what is in fact unendurable. The body itself certainly is not unendurable. It is, let us remember, the respite left by the appearance of its truth. The body awaits the revelation of its truth which when it appears will destroy it. The body is what bears the unbearable.

That is to say that incarnation is itself unbearable and the truth of the body.[12] Incarnation is a process that takes place in the body; but this unseen process is a part of its unbearable condition, it is what cannot be borne. For what is unbearable is suffering. Suffering, beyond and beneath pain, far behind pain insofar as this remains bearable, is the truth of the body, the truth of incarnation, the unbearable truth of the body. The extent of suffering veils the truth of the body because it *is* the truth and does not show it, does not disclose it at all, as it is completely identified with it.

So in relation to pleasure and pain at home in the body, suffering is the opposite of satisfaction, it is the body's truth. But it is a truth that at once hides itself and vanishes into the depths of what it does not reveal but is content with being. Suffering, then, is distinct from pain, and in a way shows this difference by rejecting it. Pain is not suffering but the nearest thing to it. It is beneath suffering and remote from it, for in this sense suffering is not painful. But we must be careful not to misunderstand the relation between them. Pain is painful because it suffers less than suffering, in the same way that suffering is not painful for it suffers more than pain. Pain suffers but it is not suffering. Consequently there is suffering in pain, pain is real, but it is not suffering, for the ordeal it experiences is not suffering—and it is this that the theorists of pain forget.

So pain is distinct from suffering exactly in the measure that the body will be distinct from incarnation; or again, pain is distinct from suffering exactly *as* the body is distinct from incarnation. It is possible to suffer while awaiting suffering, to be able to suffer though not suffering at the moment, leaving suffering remote in itself.

This term 'remote in itself' is somewhat vague, and must be returned to. This division between pain and suffering is just what we term an *absence of relationship*. Suffering bears no relation to pain.

To go back to the beginning of the debate, one can say that the relation of the believer in regard to the body is the absence of relation. But to say this is only to return to what has already been discussed and set out. I bear no relation to my body, for union with what is foreign implies an absence of relation. Two wholly foreign realities are neither in opposition nor in union—they pass into one another and remain distinct without mixing, for they become *unrelated* to one another. So the Kingdom is unrelated to the world, as incarnation is unrelated to the body. Better, this absence of relation between Kingdom and world is fulfilled in the Body, the Body of Christ, and, by adoption, the body of the believer.

That is to say that the aims of thought are first of all aims on the body and its concerns that have a bodily meaning— even the most abstract thoughts. To jump, to run, to dance, but also to speak, to count, to separate and bring together, all this is achieved by a mobilization of my bodily powers. My aims have nothing bodily in them, but they are directed to my body, for they have no meaning apart from my body.

The soul does not become incarnate, for it has always been incarnate. There is just one thing that I cannot *become*, my body as such, my bodily condition. I cannot become it, I cannot become corporeal, I cannot become incarnate, because I am already incarnate. The body is the one thing I cannot become because I am not related to it. And if I am not related, this is because I am of another kind, I am basically separate from it by a complete absence of relation, there is nothing 'in common' between us. This explains the following paradox: if you look at me, it is certainly myself that you are seeing—there is nobody else; but if I look at myself in a mirror, is it really myself that I see? Isn't it rather what anybody else would see if it happened that I was not myself?

From this we may draw one conclusion: taken in the process of incarnation, I am my body. My body is not so far from me that I can own or disown it: I am it. I am my body insofar as there is no unrelated action between us that would put it at a distance from me, that would let me separate from it or become it.

But the result of analyzing this absence of relation is this, *my body is not myself.* I am no more my body than it is what I am. My body is not myself, but the way to my mortal centre. If anyone reaches to my centre, they would have to pass by my body. But my body in itself is not me. This distinction appears in the way I am unable to grasp the complexity of organs within me. Neither the work of my heart, nor my brain, nor my liver are like my work as an incarnate being. They are altogether different. Nothing in the nervous system is like thought, despite some resemblances that are easy to refute. The complexity of organs has no meaning for me, but they have a meaning (for a biologist) foreign to what is my meaning. On the other hand I can have a meaning for them, as they can feel in their operation the meaning of the work I do as a living incarnate being—my heart can beat faster in joy or fear, I can blush or turn pale, St Francis of Assisi can receive the stigmata. When the organic body seems to have a meaning for me, as when I take a drug that produces illusions, this is because the defined ground of my body, which I use to think, has been modified.

Doubtless, in a way now well–known, it is in the context of language that the relation between my body and myself is most clearly shown. Contrary to what a phrase of Hegel's would suggest, we do not think *in* words but behind them, on the reverse side of them, in opposition to the language openly spoken—for the system of sounds, and even of words, means nothing if there is no–one to utter them. Anyhow, without this absence of relation, without the slight but flexible prop of language, meaning itself would vanish.

In an exactly similar way we may say that it is not *in* or *by* the body that we live, but behind it, unrelated to its meaningless organic elaboration. But without this absence of relation I would be lost, for I *am* just this difference in kind from my body.

This difference between my body and myself, this absence of relation which is in no way a separation or a union, shows my poverty. To be poor is not to own nothing. It is to see taken from me what I thought I had. Now the body is like that: unrelated, inaccessible. I am it, but it is also seen, and so beyond my reach. I am it and it is not me. I am poor, not rich, in my body. But this poverty gives it a value beyond price.

II. John of the Cross and his Body

What has the discussion of the body in the light of John's writings revealed?

The body is the place of incarnation. It is the movement of the Kingdom towards the world. It is opaque in appearance, visible, vulnerable, mortal, awaiting its truth in suffering. But therefore it reveals *me*, it is what I am, in the sense that the verb 'to be' is active. I am an action unrelated to the organism, not to be limited to it, although in one sense that is all it is. If I am my body, my body is not myself.

Put in these terms, the problem is not difficult to state. We have to see what in John's life allows us to see the meaning of the body. But it is a delicate matter, for there is perhaps no subject about which ideas have so much changed as attitudes to the body. In our day there has been a rehabilitation of the body unknown in the sixteenth century. So let us begin at a point where our epoch and John's agree—the body is the centre of suffering, it is what suffering is concerned with.

Suffering, in the ordinary meaning of the word, came to John when he was very young and in all its forms—hunger, illness, treachery, corporal punishment, endured by himself and by others. But there is one factor that brings together all the difficulties.

John treated his body as an enemy. The 'flesh' was for him one of the three obstacles. Clearly it is necessary to distinguish between the flesh and the body. But he imposed privations on himself. He wore a hair shirt. He beat himself. He ordered corporal punishments. It is no use saying that he did this often so as to make it less of a humiliation; it still makes us reflect.

To a monk who observed that Christ did not wear a hair shirt or impose corporal punishment on himself or others, John replied that Christ had no evil passions to mortify. An unsatisfactory reply for, to follow the argument, Christ's contemporaries had 'evil passions to mortify' yet he asked nothing of the kind of them. Suffering and martyrdom are always involuntary.

It would perhaps be too simple to explain all this by the spirit of the age. This sort of behaviour was general. We hear of a Carmelite monk who never took off his hair shirt for a whole year. But John was very able to break with his age— for instance he had only scorn for the very Spanish piety of dressing up statues and elaborately decorating oratories.

In his writings there is material for a different attitude to the body. It might be objected that this is *our* view, and that we are getting away from John. And yet mortification of the body as such finds little place in his pages—he does not seem to have paid much attention to it. Doubtless what is imposed on the body is intended to bring about reconciliation with it. But why deliberately make it suffer? Why this apparent hatred of the body? We must try hard to understand what mortification is all about.

There is one reservation, however, and this is that there seems to be a residue of platonism. And even if what we said of the soul and the body (in Chapter Six, I) is true, at moments John is carried away by the weight of his vocabulary. There is in Christianity a side that does not properly belong to it but is the mark of a strange temperamental attitude towards the relations between 'the world' and 'heaven'. 'Heaven' was not always viewed as the unseen hidden in the heart of the seen, nor eternity as the truth of time concealed in it. John opposed this tendency with strength and courage, but it had its effect on him and sometimes made his thought deviate perilously towards what was not its true nature. We have to summon John as a witness against John.

But perhaps the question has not been put correctly, or in

its historical setting. What impression did John make on his contemporaries? Like Teresa of Avila, he aroused conflicting views among the Carmelites. They knew him as a reformer who wanted to restore the original austerity of their calling. In this aspect he frightened them—some were afraid to be put in the same house as him for fear of the harsh life he would introduce. But once they were with him there was a change of perspective—then they were happy and loved him.

In fact wherever he went his first concern was not to increase, but to cut down, the penitential exercises, to relieve burdens and trials, not add to them. He it was who gave extra time for recreation and introduced more loving care. These two aspects went together. It was because his demands were pitched so high that he could afford to allow freedom. He did not compensate for his demands by gestures of friendship, no, but he was able to be liberal precisely because his demands went to the essential. Because his demands were true, authentic and in no way artificial they could go to the very limits and yet produce freedom and love.

Before returning to the question of the body and the understanding of mortification in the light of John's thought, it is important to consider a problem not yet discussed—the problem of sin.

What is sin? How is it possible to be guilty before God? Put like this, the question cannot be answered. We must revise our terms. We must not ask how to free ourselves from sin, as if it had an independent being. In fact it is so deeply hidden, so embedded in us, that not only can we not get rid of it, but it has become part of us. It is within us and we move and have our being in it. Perhaps the difficulty is not so much to separate ourselves from it as to see where it is, for the feeling of guilt is obviously no real proof of sin. Sin cannot be seen just because it is so close.

Sin does not prevent us from having a true relationship with God, from purifying our desire. We have to look at it the other way round—it is our relation to God that discloses our fault, and discloses it when we have already gone beyond it. Our awareness of sin comes only when it is forgiven. Sin is not so much what entangles us as what God's love frees us from. It frees us, and that is all that matters. But we cannot be freed unless we are freed from something. This 'something' is sin. This is the only possible and satisfying view of it. If we approach the problem from the other angle we are lost— being freed would be a hostile act. If I begin by saying 'man is a sinner' then forgiveness will never appear as a free act of grace—either it will be my right or an arbitrary favour. But with the experience of freedom and love, I can see how much alienation and lovelessness I have been saved from. Accusation of the fault must come from freedom, otherwise everything becomes false and wretched and tarnished.

So sin is separation from God. But (see Chapter Two, I) our separation from God is also our relation to him. That is why Christianity is not manichean. In Christianity separation restores the relationship through desire. Christ had to take on our sin to bring us back to the Father, and he became our separation from the Father in order to be able to unite us to him. He died on the cross and in so doing died with our sin. In him sin became both what separates us from God and what brings us to him. Yet clearly there is no question of rejoicing in sin—this would not be to rejoice in our separation, it would be not to perceive the separation as such. As separation from God *and* relationship with him, sin passes through the absolute separation of death to reach through it the absolute relationship.

So the body is linked to sin because it is what dies, it is where death and resurrection take place (and in strict logic this can only be a resurrection of the body). So it is wide of the mark to say that the body is sin. In fact it is the place where God leaves us, the place where the whole story of our adoption as sons happens. It is not the flesh that binds us and leads us towards earthly things when we should be making ourselves at home in our fatherland in heaven, but rather that element in us that faces death.

To hate the body is to mistake the victim for the guilty, and this would bring a real and bitter attempt to mortify the body. Now is the moment to try to show how this would be enjoyment of the body by making it suffer.

This possible perversion of the mortified body is called masochism. In this I give myself the satisfaction of disowning my body by suppressing it. I give myself pleasure with suffering, because suffering shows me, not my separation from myself, but just how much I exist in my body here present.

In sadism or masochism I rejoice in the vulnerability of the body and want to make myself or someone else at home in it. That too is why sado–masochism can be a way of sexual satisfaction. By inflicting torture on myself or another, I am not changing myself or another into a 'thing', to enjoy my freedom, as is often said. What I am doing is much more perverse: I am asserting not only that I am my body, but that my body is myself (see Chapter Six, I). Similarly I am asserting not only that the other is his body, but that his body is himself—he is nowhere else. So the unfathomable interior separation that gives meaning to me and my body is annulled. Sado–masochism is the greatest of all perversions, for it maintains that the body is not separate, but just the individual himself.

A mortification based on these assumptions would be no more or less than a rejection of salvation. For hatred of the body can only go in the same direction as masochism. It is not hatred of sin but love of sin. It reminds my body that it is not separate, but here, resting in itself. If I hate my body it is because I want no more to do with it. I want no more of my separated state. But if I do not want my separation, I do not want God. To make my own or another's body suffer for the sake of suffering is the complete denial of God.

Perhaps we can now understand the strange relationship between John and mortification. To mortify the body is not a *means* of reaching God, it is a *consequence* of the relationship with God. It is in the context of the relationship with the desired and desiring Absolute that mortification has to be seen. It must be seen in the context of love for God and love for the suffering body of Christ.

Here too we must guard against a view of mortification that involves a suspect element of passion—wanting to make my body become Christ's suffering body so as to identify myself with him and become in fact as adorable as he is. There can be no question of shaping the body to that of the suffering Son.

Nevertheless, at the heart of desire, mortification should reveal the suffering of being separated from God. Mortification is not a way of increasing my suffering, but of lessening it, by making my body feel the pain that is bearable as opposed to the suffering that is unbearable (see Chapter Six, I).

It would be inexact to claim that the man who bites his fist because his suffering is too much for him is trying to increase his suffering. Mortification quietens suffering—not intellectual or moral suffering, but spiritual suffering, that is to say of the whole man, body and spirit together.

Despite some unhappy verbal confusions, it is possible to see a sense in which we can talk of mortifying bodily passions. It is to take part in the struggle against sin. It is a struggle against 'the passions of the body'—the body which cannot bear spiritual suffering, which would prefer to quit the place where it ought to be, return to easier tasks, give up the fight. And if Christ's contemporaries knew nothing of this kind of mortification, it was precisely because they had him with them. But 'Jesus said to them, "Can the wedding guests fast while the bridegroom is with them? As long as they have the bridegroom with them, they cannot fast. The days will come, when the bridegroom is taken away from them, and then they will fast in that day" '.[1]

Seen in this way, mortification is not morbid. It cannot be looked at in itself or considered alone. Nor is it possible to get close enough to it to examine it. This is why there is no mention of the benefits of the hair shirt or the scourge in John's writings. Suffering in face of sin can be such that the scourge has to be used to endure it. But it cannot be put forward as a means in itself, in the same way as one might recommend, for example, a reading of the gospels or the poems of John of the Cross.

What is mortification? A drop into the great darkness at the heart of the night itself, where pain is summoned as a remedy for suffering. Anyone who mortified himself to suffer, instead of to suffer less, would be perverse indeed.

For though suffering has to be faced, it has not to be sought. John never sought it. He wrote a distraught letter to Catalina of Jesus, asking her to help him as a friend by praying God for an end to his suffering. And there is a letter of Teresa's in which she asks for prayers for John, for he was much troubled and 'has had enough suffering'.[2] Because suffering is the truth of the body it cannot be sought. It reaches its full meaning when it is passively received, accepted and welcomed—in the darkest night, which alone allows the light to be seen as it reverses the meaning of darkness and makes death the place of life itself.

CONCLUSION

'To love is to forgive, but to forgive is not what one thinks'

The body is the mortal centre of the soul, its basic passivity and poverty.

To sum up the ground covered: man is all the more human, all the more a being of desire dependent on his own strength, for his nature being at a desiring distance from God. If desire can be seen as man's centre, this is insofar as man gives himself up to an absolute word, where he is in relation to what is not human, to God. The summons of the Absolute lets man escape from his destined limits because it imposes man's limits on himself in a specific way. Man is wholly man because God is wholly God.

In conclusion it is necessary to define the relations between man and the Absolute. The Absolute comes to man through a Word that has taken hold of him, set him up in his independence and in his limits, thereby achieving a radical opening, for in him there opens the revelation of an elsewhere. God is active, man is passive.

But unfortunately this simple view is too simple. Certainly man has a complete passivity that is his poverty, his body. But the soul that is this body exists unrelated to it and is not passive. Man's passivity is in fact the highest activity, that of creation and discovery.

How do these two activities come together? Two demands have to be respected:

1. God's activity is directed towards the human will as such.

2. Similarly the human will goes towards God and can only aim at him because he is supremely active and can in no way be assimilated. Human will is directed towards God's activity inasmuch as this activity escapes it. ?

What, therefore, is the meaning of the phrase: 'To do God's Will'.

To consider this requires investigating the idea of obedience. But we have to start by rejecting one meaning of the word. To obey does *not* mean to be under someone else's domination. Certainly to be obedient *can* mean 'to be submissive' or 'to bow before the will of another', but we mean *free* obedience to another's will, not the result of a trial of strength in which one gives way to the other.

To all appearances, to do the will of God is to obey him, yet this must not be said too hastily, before what it means is properly understood. In fact if the word 'obedience' has a straightforward meaning when it is a matter of one person obeying another, it is by no means certain that it would have the same meaning when the will to be obeyed is that of the otherness of God.

What does it mean to obey another human being? When I obey a human being, his will is not imposed on me but offered to me. The human will does not really know what it wants—it is only in textbooks that it pursues a goal known in advance; rather than the pursuit of a specific goal, it is bringing into effect the means that shall disclose it. It is bringing the means into effect that teach the will what it wants; in the same way it is the process of disclosing what it is looking for that enables it to increase its grasp of the means. From that point of view the man who obeys is one of the means put into effect by the man who commands. So the man who obeys takes part, as a means, in disclosing the will that he serves. Without any paradox it is possible to say that it is insofar as he reveals the other's will that he does what is wanted.

I am then in a sense the master of the will I serve. The process by which I accept the other's command, and respond to what he wants, brings my will into the realm of his freedom. Only my freedom can set me to serve another's freedom. So respect for his freedom guarantees mine. By seeing him as free, I give myself the freedom to decide what he wants of me.

This control over the will that is offered to me is—to say the least—a far cry from any kind of domination. That is why a vow of obedience is one of freedom, not slavery, as it puts me in the supremely free position of allowing the other to speak, and take back what he says as he likes, and not as I like, but without surrendering any of my independence.

Taken this way, obedience requires two conditions. First an order has to be given, a demand has to be stated, in a way that can be seen. Certainly there can be a discrepancy of varying degrees between the way it is seen and the demand itself, but no matter—the essential is that it should be put forward here and now and seen as given to the one who has to respond to it, either because it is addressed to him or because he thinks it is.

But the idea of obedience can be considered away from any concern with the idea of hierarchy. This might indeed be the moment to consider hierarchy, perhaps especially as a service rendered rather than an order that constricts, but this would take us beyond our scope. Nevertheless it should be made plain that 'the man who commands' could be any human being: for instance a poor man, one who has nothing and whose very destitution is a summons and a command, can well be the master in a relationship of obedience. On the other hand, in the case of a man with power and wealth giving the command one should proceed with more caution and carefully consider the words used—laying still more emphasis on the freedom of the man who obeys, so that obedience is given its full value.

In any case, what is demanded has to come before what is given. A definite statement not heard before has to be put forward. It is important that one should be able to obey a man capable of taking back what has been done, of saying 'yes' or 'no' to what is given to him. The man who is served has a right to respect. Obedience has to be kept up so that he can take what he wants from what we give him.

This requirement from someone endowed with the power to judge what is given him is justified in this way: we obey only a spoken word. And we only obey a word that is being spoken now, not one that has been spoken in the past, for only now can we understand what is uttered and put forward our questions, only now can we see its point of origin, and that this is the point where it is obeyed. In order for the word to have a meaning it must refer to the person who speaks it, apart from what he says. Hence a body is needed for a word, a body that speaks it, that brings it to light, yet is not it. There is no person who speaks and can be obeyed—in the sense shown here—unless his word is uttered by a body which is not the word itself.

The second condition for obedience could be summed up as follows: through his power to judge, the point of origin of the word must be completely definite, whereas its meaning can be relatively indefinite. The one who listens gives meaning to what is said. But he does so insofar as this comes from outside, disclosing what is other but not confused with it. The word is accepted, taken in, because its origin is not. It is because the origin is so definite that the meaning is not. Similarly the meaning is indefinite (up to a point) and therefore its origin is definite. Many people experience this without recognizing it. Observing that to understand someone is never to understand what he is, but only what he says, they think they are faced with a failure to communicate, whereas they have the conditions for genuine communication.

But this definition of the meaning would be impossible if the man to be obeyed knew exactly what he wanted, if he knew exactly what he was saying. It is important that he should be able to recognize with astonishment that what he has been given is what he really wanted.

Can this idea of obedience be used to throw light on obedience to God? Neither of the required conditions operates here.

Certainly the commandment has been given as revelation clearly shows. But no-one has seen the Father except the Son.[1] It is true that he who sees the Son sees the Father[2]—but the Son is dead and risen, the uttering of the Word has been silenced and can no longer be found except in the ecclesiastical community. If God is present in the Church and the believer, then this is in the course of history and in the vicissitudes of their lives, not in a statement given directly to anybody (not even to the Pope). Christ's body in the eucharist is a body offered up, not a body that speaks. To do God's will would not be to obey a word rising up before the believer and calling to him, as has been too lightly said.

The second condition fares no better. Here the *meaning* is not indefinite—the Word, *as meaning*, is definite and this is why it does not answer back or reply to those who serve it for

good or ill. There can be no question of giving God's Word
its meaning. When a believer reads the Bible, it is certainly
he who reads the text and clarifies his faith by his attention
to the verses, but in fact it is much more the text that reads
the believer, quietly taking into account his interpreation and
giving him its meaning. As Pierre Magnard[3] said, 'Is it really
the man who has read the book? Is it not rather the book that
has deciphered the man?'

So God's will cannot be obeyed in that way. And yet the
conditions for obedience have their bearing here, provided
that we note that the believer does not obey God but, paradoxically, it is God who offers his obedience to the believer
without any loss of his divinity. This defines the believer's
position before God, and allows us to suppose that it is certainly not he who gives an order to God, but the Man of
Poverty, the one who demands with all his being, with everything that he is.

Since what is at issue in obedience concerns a word, we
must get back to the heart of God's Word. What do we mean
when we say that God is a God who speaks? The God in
question is a God who has spoken and is now silent.

> One word spake the Father, which Word was His Son, and
> this Word He speaks ever in eternal silence, and in silence
> must it be heard by the soul.[4]

Now the man who has said what he had to say and still
stands by waits in the attentive silence of a listener. God
listens. The soul listening to God's silence is simply listening
to a listener. Not that God is passive, or less than the lord of
history, or less than the highest activity in the depths of the
believer's will, but it is his silence and his care that are active.

God's activity has to be viewed as the silence of a supreme
care. That is why when the soul reaches divine union, it is
only to the soul that the Beloved's *words* are addressed:

> It believes that He has no other soul in the world to favour
> thus, nor aught else wherewith to occupy Himself, but that
> He is wholly for itself alone.[5]

In fact what the Beloved says is not a declaration but the
very silence of the care he lavishes on the soul. That is why
the soul knows it is unique and favoured above all others; if

words were uttered they would proclaim the distance between creatures where it becomes possible to compare them, whereas loving care unfolds with no comparison and is given only to one. If this care took the form not of silence but of a word, then this last quotation from John could not even be imagined.

So God's Will is the acceptance offered to the believer's will, and although this cannot obey God in the sense commonly used in human relations, the phrase 'to do the Will of God' now has its content. It is the will's acceptance of the infinite Patience that listens to it. In agreeing to be heard, that is to say in accepting its true meaning without prejudice—very far from what it itself can know—the will surrenders giving itself a meaning and accepts that what it does should be threaded into a plan other than its own. So the believer has faith in the inconceivable humility of God who takes his human will so as to make of it a truth that he could never have guessed. God makes himself humble and takes the human will into his sovereignty. To sum up, doing God's will means knowing and wanting one's will to be used by God as he wishes.

The truth that comes from God is neither an addition nor an explanation. It is not an addition in the sense of being simply superimposed on the human will, offering a meaning other than man wants—that would be too automatic, God would seem active, and man nothing but passivity.

But neither is it an explanation of what man wants, the disclosure of what he in fact wanted. That would imply a return to the idea of God as a part of man, a God who was no more than an object of man's desire, not a living God who speaks to man's desire and transforms it into something divine—God whose thoughts are never those of men. His taking over of the will occurs, but there is no sign of what happens, or of how it happens, or of what exactly is the meaning and fate of actions so taken over by God.

So it is necessary to analyze the nature of God's obedience to man, and try to give it another name to express more exactly what it is. It concerns a truth that is other, that challenges mine, yet does not necessarily destroy it in the way that truth destroys error—on the contrary, it strengthens it in its process.

Here the abyss of guilt might well open before us. Always at odds with God's will, none of my actions is what God wants, so my whole life is on the way to being condemned, its salvation wholly dependent on an arbitrary divine grace from outside, and without any possible reference to works. Such an idea may respect divine freedom, but it overlooks God's humility which welcomes actions insofar as they are willed by man.

But there is an abyss on the other side which gives no better chance of understanding the process—the assurance that whatever I do is good since it is taken up by God. In that case I would only have to be true to myself and pay no attention to ethical or other considerations outside my actions. The fact that the infinite meaning of God would be involved in what I do would no longer seem as a claim over me by God, but as something taken for granted, corresponding to the inner nature of my actions.

We can only bring agreement between the two wills by admitting their discrepancy. Whatever I do, my actions are not God's, but are to be taken up by him in some way that is not disclosed, and that is how I want them to be. The will hands over what it wants to the handling of another will beyond it. It finds consolation in the process by which it surrenders itself. Further, the will wants God to be free. It feels that what allows it to act is precisely that God can take up its actions and alter their meaning. We have to see that the consolation we receive from the divine will is simply our satisfaction in the certainty that our actions, however trivial, do not hinder divine activity, and that insofar as I act like this, my action will be favoured and transformed in such a way that it becomes open to the breath of the Spirit.

So the action of the will finds its meaning in superabundant measure. Its meaning goes infinitely beyond itself, it cannot be cut down to what it is, but is given a totality of meaning. This meaning is a long way from any categories I could assign to it myself, for these are nothing compared with what it receives through grace. We see how wrong it would be to think that our many different actions are somehow on the same level, inasmuch as they are destined to be taken up by God and inasmuch as they are one undifferentiated substance. No, we have to see clearly that in this perspective the reality of actions is strengthened. History is made out of just such a series of events. What God takes up are happenings freely brought about by man, so any specific historical event is endowed with its infinite meaning. And if we cannot believe that it is in our power to set obstacles in God's way, yet the ups and downs of human actions engage man's full responsibility. The suffering that I have spread around me finds its meaning beforehand in the cross and a greater wealth of meaning in the resurrection, but it remains suffering all the same, and suffering brought about by me.

Once we have said this, but only then, we can agree with John in describing the Spirit's task as giving the good and evil in me the same savour—'Taste conforms to no set laws'.[6]

As a result of this, God's whole being seems to be *forgiveness*, for in fact the task of forgiveness is not to eliminate wrong but to take it up. Forgiveness does not say, or does not only say, 'you didn't want to do that', or, with Socrates, 'no–one does evil deliberately'. Forgiveness is aware of this aspect but is not founded on it. Forgiveness is above all a refusal to judge. And in this context there are two points which throw light on obedience.

1. Forgiveness pinpoints the origin of an action. It refuses to reduce the will to its action. It forgives, that is to say it separates the will from its action, not by dividing the action from the will—for every action has clearly been willed—but from the force of the will taken as a whole. It emphasizes the distinction between will and action. This is where forgiveness is original—bearing on the fact that the will is not simply how it shows itself in action but lives in the difference between itself and what it does. So forgiveness goes down to the origin of action due to its freedom with regard to it and hence its power to dissociate itself from any action, however crushing it may be.

2. Seen from another point of view, forgiveness decides the meaning of what is done. It gives a new meaning to it, different from the one given it by the will. Action, having enslaved the will, *can* imply its freedom, provided that this new meaning—an unforeseen act of grace—is held out to it. To quote Emmanuel Lévinas: 'A being capable of another fate than its own is fruitful . . . this victory in the time of fruitfulness . . . is forgiveness'.[7] It is by making sterile actions fruitful

that God's forgiveness is best revealed. But it is not only some actions that are sterile—all actions are sterile for all involve risk, and none of them contains in itself the promise of its own effectiveness.

The one who forgives gives a meaning to the action of the one who is forgiven. Thus the one who is forgiven is like a man who gives a command that he himself has never ordered. But that is a glorious form of obedience. The action that is forgiven is not obliterated, not even as having been done in ignorance, but glorified.

Yet forgiveness can only be granted to actions already done—there can be no forgiveness before an action is done. Failure to understand this was the perversion of Prince Myshkin in *The Idiot*. The idiot is not an image of Christ but a painful caricature of him. And there was something diabolical in Myshkin—he forgave before the act was committed. He loved the sinner, but not only the one who *had* sinned, but the one who *was going to sin*. So he loved the sin. In this way he aroused in those he met a taste for salvation and its effective loss.[8]

So we come to the final question.

How is it possible to get back to the taking over of my will by God? How are we to understand, on the level of my will, the absolute distinction between the believer's will and God's will?

It is a matter of grasping in a human way the true being of God. This formula will upset only those who do not know the meaning that the mystic gives to it. It is the fact that God cannot be brought down to the level of human desire that makes it possible to say this. Thanks to the distance between God and the believer—which enables God to be in the believer—we can regard the human condition in this way. We are talking about a human idea whose possibilities are not human—the idea of theocentric man.

The surrender of the human will to God's will, the meaning of the phrase 'to do the will of God', can then be taken in the human sense of will.

We have seen that the will is what sets in motion the means by which it uncovers its objective and what it wants. It can also be said that the will wants itself, it wants its own disclosure through what it achieves. So it always discloses the whole of itself in the least of its designs. But it cannot see itself—what it sees is what it wants. Neither in things nor in itself can the will have a real meaning unless it sees *itself* in its object—which is not itself yet which gives it form—just because the will wants it. For the will to define itself it only has to say what it wants—which is not itself. But here there is a gap in the exercise of the will—in relation to its own basis it never goes back on itself. The will is unrelated to itself so cannot grasp itself. It knows itself only on the surface, but what it sees coming to the surface is its own hidden depth, the sum of what it basically is.

It is in these depths that the will renounces itself and becomes open to the possibility of being taken up by an Other.

The task then is to consider the relationship, in those depths, between the two wills contained in my will when it accepts this difference, that is to say when it sees that it has been taken over. For in fact of itself it can only be aware of itself in the infinitely dispersed particularity of what it wants.

So one might say that the will that has accepted its inner difference is a fragmented will, while at the same time discerning its unity—not the unity that it seeks when active, but the unity already granted before it sets to work, when it agrees never to dominate what it produces, remaining all the more voluntary because it *wants* the full meaning of what it does to elude it.

To wish that my will were no longer mine could only come about through real obedience to another will. But we do not obey God, though it is possible to obey others. It is only in the exercise of obedience as described here that the will can learn of a self–surrender that is not a break in its mastership.

Obedience to others offers a lesson that we should think about. It teaches that obedience is not automatic, that it is not natural to obey. The idea of others having to be obeyed is not one that is taken for granted. To perceive that I should have to recognize the other's freedom, which is his otherness. But this does not come of itself. I cannot force myself to see it. I see the otherness of something when I say, 'it happens that . . .', which shows my life as a series of happenings. Then the other seems very near and at the same time completely foreign. It seems close, but in its very otherness. The spontaneous origin of the other is foreign, cannot be reached or defined, so is infinitely far away. So the process of obedience consists in going infinitely close for the sake of going infinitely far away. But this of course is typical of love. Love is nothing but the consummation of this process.

If we look again from this angle at what has been said, we can now say that I can only obey when I love. Love is the necessary condition of obedience, as obedience is the effect of love.

But what is love?

· The act of obedience demands taking into account the native will of another, and love therefore demands the surrender of what I am doing, and the acceptance of my will as master, yes, but only insofar as it is the other's will that gives the orders. But this surrender is only understood if I also know that the origin of what I do is distinct from what I do in fact. Without that I would be unable to obey, and the other's will would be changed not into a will that is obeyed but into a will that dominates or is dominated. Without love obedience is impossible and becomes a struggle for power. So to love is to disclose in myself that distance between my actions and their origin that I have noticed in the beloved other.

So the question becomes urgent: who is going to bring about this disclosure in me? In fact this break within my will, which is a condition of all the rest, is part of the free gift that marks love for others. It is this quality of free gift which accounts for the free gift of love. It is tempting to answer the question by saying that the disclosure is brought about by the love for me that a brother has or could have. As freedom awakens freedom, so love awakens love, and for the same reason.

But that is only partly true, not the final truth. The possibility for love to embrace and awaken love must be based elsewhere. We cannot go round in a circle for it might involve a perversion—left to itself, it might invite dependence. If I learn my freedom and my peace from my brother, I become dependent on him and need him in order to exist. So the answer to our question could be accepted only under certain conditions which would break the circle. Otherwise passionate love—which is neither love nor the truth of desire, for it dreams of satisfaction—would keep people gravitating in a closed circle. Dependence would come up against spontaneity, and so, by a trick well–known to any analyst of passion, lead to a narcissism which should be shunned.

Whereas it is independence that obedience really conceals in its depths, spontaneity, the distinction between the origin and the action, can only be understood as the independence of brothers among each other. Moreover, this independence is a demand of high quality and is lived out in suffering. If I learn independence from my brother, and if I learn from love itself his complete independence, then this will involve me in frustration. How pleasant it would be if the other were myself! What I can do for my brother, even in obeying him, is little; my will, my clumsy will, with its own strength can only want to take the place of his, unless it is left to its own inclination which is to get the other to acknowledge it. The will wants the illusion of knowing that it could be free even in its alienation. All I can do for the other, then, is to suffer from my inability to do anything, that is to say to turn to the taking–up of my actions by the loving will of the Father who made us brothers. In other words I can do nothing for my brother unless I change myself. (Obviously this does not entail a refusal to act on his behalf—quite the reverse).

So the possibility of love—this 'disclosure' in me—must be placed elsewhere than in the awakening of brotherly love by the love that a brother has or could have for me. Note, however, to escape from the circle, that the inner disclosure is clearer, the peace deeper, in both myself and the other, when I do not expect love from my brother. The disclosure only really comes into being through a curious indifference to what my brother thinks of me, even in the heart of love. The process of respect for the other's will that goes with obedience signifies a trust in him, giving him back to himself. Anxiety for the other's salvation is contrary to true love. Peace is revealed much more when I leave the other to himself and expect nothing from him, no more than the chance of serving him in a fitting way.

This analysis of trust in the other, this basic refusal to take his place, does not exclude the chance of reciprocity. But it shows that this cannot be passionate, and that a certain form of reciprocity, far from lessening independence, increases it.

It is reciprocity where every time the other recognizes me I at once respond by recognizing him; but this process cannot be fulfilled unless the will of *one* is broken and forgiven.

Here one can discern the outline of an Other, who is not the human other. For by its precedence in relation to others, and by its contingency, the disclosure of my will cannot be made the responsibility of myself or of others. It was not always already there within me, but is a gift from the absolute Other. The place of the Other, in whom revelation summons us to recognize God, is the disclosure itself, that which lies between the origin and the action.

A time of silence impels my surrender and severs the ties which connect my will with my actions. So it is death that comes to make itself at home in the deepest recess of my being. But death is what frees love, since then nothing can prevent my actions coming under another will—whether a brother's or God's. In this respect, death seems no less than the taking–up of my will by that of God.

But this time of silence is not content with fostering brotherly love. It is not only a taking–up of ourselves, but is able to grow, nourished by the love it produces, and it accepts this love because it is its own creation. Without any change (for it is not clear what such a change could mean) it is deepened by all the human love that crosses it. This silence becomes deeper as the brother who brings it into being is not others in general but a concrete being who makes his own demands.

In seeking to grasp the import of what mysticism has taught us, there are two points to be made. The first concerns faith. If what has been said is correct and rests on John's thought, then it seems that faith cannot do without charity which reveals faith's human conditions, just as faith reveals the human conditions of charity.

The second is more directly human: there is no love that does not pass through death, for what discloses the inner gap of the will, and enables domination to be re–absorbed, is the complete self–surrender of the will, the silence that separates the origin of the action from the action itself. It truly concerns death, for it is what we know nothing of, apart from its omnipresence which penetrates our enclosed selves, telling us that we have already lost everything and that in this lies the joy of our capacity to desire.

NOTES

N.B. For all references to the works of St John of the Cross, cf. *The Complete Works of Saint John of the Cross, doctor of the Church*, edited by E. Allison Peers, in 3 volumes. Published by Burns Oates, London, 1943. See list on pages 12–13.

Introduction

1. *Ascent*, prologue, par. 9. (Vol. I, p. 15).
2. This is not in contradiction to what is written above. Sometimes to respect the life and thought of others is to give it more value than they do themselves.
3. *Points of Love*, no. 36. (Vol. III, p. 253).

Chapter One

I. What is Mysticism?

1. G. Morel, *Le Sens de l'existence selon saint Jean de la Croix* (Aubier, 1960).
2. This word is used despite its imprecision because it is the word John uses. Here 'man' would do equally well. It is with the whole of himself that the believer is called to make the journey.
3. *Ascent*, Book II, chap. 17, par. 4. (Vol. I, p. 139).
4. *ibid.*, chap. 16, par. 14. (Vol. I, p. 137).
5. *ibid.*, chap. 4, par. 5. (Vol. I, p. 76).
6. *ibid.*, chap. 9, par. 1. (Vol. I, p. 98).
7. *ibid.* (Vol. I, p. 98).
8. Nothing to do with the opposition between faith and reason. Faith is thinkable, with the whole of what that implies. The 'known' that is rejected here is that which claims to *have mastery*

over its object. We do not believe in God as we know that 2 + 2 = 4.

9. *Ascent*, Book II, chap. 22, par. 5. (Vol. I. p. 175).
10. *Spiritual Canticle*, stanza 28, par. 1. (Vol. II, pp. 143–4).
11. *ibid*. (Vol. II, p. 144).
12. *Ascent*, Book II, chap. 22, par. 9. (Vol. I, p. 177).
13. Let us note, however, that there was no contempt for reason with John.
14. *Ascent*, Book II, chap. 4, par. 4. (Vol. I, p. 75).
15. *ibid*., chap. 7, par. 5. (Vol. I, p. 89).
16. *Dark Night*, Book II, chap. 7, par. 5. (Vol. I, pp. 414–15).
17. The newness of the mystical journey is not in contradiction to what has already been said about its analytical character. It is in terms of explicit knowledge that there is no 'progress' regarding the revelation made to the Church. Whereas the believer's self–deepening through what he knows in faith can cause fundamental changes.
18. *Dark Night*, Book II, chap. 16, par. 8. (Vol. I, p. 452).
19. *Ascent*, Book II, chap. 22, par. 15. (Vol. I, pp. 181–2).

II. *John as Spiritual Director*

1. The order's full name is The Order of Our Lady of Mount Carmel.
2. Cf. Chapter One, I.
3. *Ascent*, Book II, chap. 18, par. 5. (Vol. I, p. 146).
4. E. Lévinas, *Totalité et Infini*.
5. *Ascent*, Book II, chap. 18, par. 8. (Vol. I, p. 148).
6. *Dark Night*, Book I, chap. 7, par. 3. (Vol. I, p. 369).
7. *ibid*., Book II, chap. 7, par. 3. (Vol. I, p. 415).
8. *Spiritual Sentences and Maxims*, no. 14. (Vol. III, p. 242).
9. *ibid*., no. 15. (Vol. III, p. 242).
10. *Points of Love*, no. 13. (Vol. III, p. 251).
11. *Spiritual Sentences and Maxims*, nos. 25/26. (Vol. III, p. 244).
12. *Points of Love*, no. 13. (Vol. III, p. 251).
13. *Cautions*, no. 12. (Vol. III, p. 224).
14. *Spiritual Sayings*, nos. 12 and 13. (Vol. III, pp. 314–15).
15. *Points of Love*, no. 56. (Vol. III, p. 255).
16. *Spiritual Sentences and Maxims*, no. 30. (Vol. III, p. 252).
17. *ibid*., no. 61(4). (Vol. III, p. 256).
18. *Counsels to a Religious*, no. 2. (Vol. III, p. 228).
19. *Spiritual Sentences and Maxims*, no. 31. (Vol. III, p. 252).
20. *ibid*., no. 32. (Vol. III, p. 252).
21. *Other Maxims*, no. 9, (Vol. III, p. 259).

22. *Spiritual Sayings*, no. 6. (Vol. III, p. 313).
23. Said with particular reference to a nun who had forgotten to put the 'corporal' on the altar where John was going to say mass and was afraid of Teresa's reprimand.

Chapter Two

I. God's Absence is still God

1. *Dark Night*, Book II, chap. 6, par. 1. (Vol. I, p. 409).
2. *Living Flame*, stanza 2, par. 21. (Vol. III, p. 151).
3. *Apocalypse*, 2.17.
4. *Living Flame*, stanza 2, par. 36. (Vol. III, p. 161).
5. *ibid.*, stanza 3, par. 6. (Vol. III, p. 164).
6. *ibid.*, par. 78. (Vol. III, p. 204).
7. *ibid.* (Vol. III. p. 205).
8. *Spiritual Canticle*, stanza 39, par. 3. (Vol. II, p. 396).
9. *Ascent*, Book II, chap. 5, par. 5. (Vol. I, p. 81).
10. *ibid.*, par. 6. (Vol. I, p. 82).
11. *Spiritual Canticle*, stanzas 13 and 14, par. 9. (Vol. II, p. 79).
12. *Living Flame*, verse 1. (Vol. III, p. 18).
13. *ibid.*, stanza 4, par. 4. (Vol. III, p. 214).
14. Cf. *Psalms*, no. 42–43. 'As a hart longs for flowing streams, so longs my soul for thee, O God'. The psalms are attributed to David, king of Israel (1015–975 B.C.), one of the most sympathetic and human figures in the history of Israel.
15. *Living Flame*, stanza 3, par. 19. (Vol. III, p. 172).
16. *ibid.*, par. 20. (Vol. III, p. 172).
17. *ibid.*, par. 21. (Vol. III, p. 172).
18. *ibid.*, par. 22. (Vol. III, p. 172).
19. *ibid.*, stanza 1, par. 27. (Vol. III. p. 133).
20. *ibid.*, stanza 3, par. 23. (Vol. III, p. 173). 'But seeing it is certain that, when the soul desires God with entire truth, it already (as S. Gregory says in writing of S. John [the Evangelist]) possesses Him whom it loves, how comes it, O God, that it yearns for Him Whom it already possesses?'
21. *Isaiah*, 55.8: 'For my thoughts are not your thoughts, neither are your ways my ways, says the Lord'.
22. *Dark Night*, Book 2, chap. 18. par. 2. (Vol. I, p. 461).

II. John of the Cross and God's Absence

1. *Poems*, VIII. (Vol. II, p. 454).
2. The opening words of Psalm 22 and said by Christ on the cross according to Matthew 27.46 and Mark 15.34.

Chapter Three

I. Desire

1. *Ascent*, Book I, chap. 1, par. 1. (Vol. I, p. 17).
2. *Summa Theologica*, Ia–IIa, Qu. 28 ad respondeo et ad tertium.
3. *Ascent*, Book I, chap. 4, par. 3. (Vol. I, p. 24).
4. *ibid.*, chap. 9, par. 1. (Vol. I, p. 45).
5. *ibid.* (Vol. I, p. 46).
6. *ibid.* 'Traces of soot would defile a face that is very lovely and perfect.'
7. E. Lévinas, *Totalité et Infini*, II, chap. 3.
8. *Ascent*, Book I, chap. 13, par 6. (Vol. I, p. 61).
9. *ibid.*, Book II, chap. 1, par. 1. (Vol. I, p. 66).
10. See Chapter Two, I.
11. *Ascent*, Book II, chap. 15, par. 4. (Vol. I, p. 129).
12. The reference is to what John calls 'spiritual illuminations' (*Ascent*, II, 24), interior words uttered with the aid of the Holy Spirit (*ibid.*, chap. 29), 'formal words' (*ibid.*, chap. 30), 'interior feelings' (*ibid.*, chap. 32), 'apprehensions of the memory' (*ibid.*, III, 2), 'affections of the will' (*ibid*, chap. 17).
13. *Ascent*, Book III, chap. 20, par. 2. (Vol. I, p. 272).
14. Cf. Mark 10.29–30. '. . . there is no–one who has left house or brothers or sisters or mother or father or children or lands, for my sake and for the gospel, who will not receive a hundredfold now in this time'.
15. *Ascent*, Book III, chap. 26, par. 5. (Vol. I, p. 288).
16. *ibid*
17. *Dark Night*, Book I, chap. 2, par. 6. (Vol. I, p. 355).
18. *ibid.*, par. 7. (Vol. I, p. 355).
19. *ibid.*, Book II, chap. 25, par. 4. (Vol. I, pp. 485–6).
20. Augustine, *Confessions*, Book X.6. (Penguin Classics, p. 212).
21. *Spiritual Canticle*, stanza 11, par. 6. (Vol. II, p. 241).
22. *ibid.*, stanzas 13 and 14, par. 9. (Vol. II, p. 79).
23. *ibid.*, stanza 28, par. 8. (Vol. II, p. 344).
24. *Living Flame*, prologue, par. 4. (Vol. III, p. 115).
25. *ibid.*, stanza 4, par. 16. (Vol. II, p. 215).

II. John of the Cross—a Being of Desire

1. See Conclusion.
2. *John*, 1st Epistle, 4.20.
3. *Ascent*, Book III, chap. 24, par. 4. (Vol. I, p. 283).
4. An anecdote has been recorded on this subject. Teresa liked large hosts (for holy communion) but John did not approve of

this. He probably regarded it as a sort of spiritual infantilism, or some residual superstition, or again as a disproportionate attachment to inessentials. On 18 November 1572 he gave her half a host at communion.

5. *Living Flame*, prologue. (Vol. III, p. 15).
6. The definition of a caress in E. Lévinas, *Totalité et Infini*.
7. The phrase is suggested by Simone Weil, *Gravity and Grace*.

Chapter Four

I. To Desire God provides a Meaning, but an Unexpected One

1. This means that God is not an object to the world: he is the One who *speaks*, or more exactly has spoken. Nothing could be further from this thought than a God who only exists in our subjectivity, who only exists in his relationship with us—in a word, a God who is not transcendent.
2. *Spiritual Canticle*, stanza 9, par. 5. (Vol. II, p. 61).
3. *Poems*, XIX, line 1. (Vol. II, p. 467).
4. *ibid.*, verse 3. (Vol. II, p. 468).
5. *Spiritual Canticle*, stanza 18, par. 5. (Vol. II, p. 110).
6. *ibid.*, stanza 27, par. 2. (Vol. II, p. 173).
7. *Ascent*, Book II, chap. 21, par. 1. (Vol. I, p. 218). John understands by this suggestive phrase the words that can come into the mind, or that we could read, or that others could say, and that we not only take in but are transformed by.
8. *Ascent*, Book II, chap. 32, par. 4. (Vol. I, p. 223).
9. *Dark Night*, Book I, chap. 9, par. 2. (Vol. I, p. 376).
10. *Jeremiah*, 18.6.
11. *Dark Night*, Book II, chap. 12, par. 7. (Vol. I, p. 437).
12. *ibid.*, chap. 3, par. 2. (Vol. I, p. 403).
13. *ibid.*, chap. 16, par. 8. (Vol. I, p. 452).
14. *Spiritual Canticle*, stanza 9, par. 7. (Vol. II, p. 233).
15. Kierkegaard, *Fear and Trembling*.

II. Chronological Table of John's Active Life

1. Our vital source, among others, for the information contained here is the section on John's life in: Crisógono de Jesus, O.C.D., *Vida y Obras de San Juan de la Cruz* (Madrid, 1964).

Chapter Five

I. *The World and the Kingdom*

1. Paul Ricoeur, *Philosophie de la Volonté*, vol. I, *Le Volontaire et l'Involontaire*, p. 11.
2. *John*, 18.36.
3. *Mark*, 1.15.
4. Michel Henry, *L'Essence de la manifestation*, vol. II, p. 568.
5. André Malraux, *Les Conquérants* ('Pleiades'), p. 143.
6. The disciples interpreted prophecies on the Messiah as fore-telling the political reunion of Israel. They had to go a long way to find out what sort of a kingdom was really in question. Cf. *Acts*, 1.6.
7. Whether primacy should be given to practice over theory, or theory over practice, is a celebrated dispute. But it is pointless. The meaning of theory is bounded by action, action by theory. A theory is worth no more than the possibility of action that it discloses, an action is worth no more than its meaning, and its final meaning is the disclosure of an idea. In the end a theory cannot be absolute. On the other hand, if an action cannot be absolute either, at least it can have an absolute basis and beginning. Christianity takes this demand in its exact sense. That is to say that Christian action, having its roots in the Kingdom and taking the world as its only ground of action, has nothing to envy any kind of materialism: it is not an idealism that considers 'heaven' more real than 'Earth'.
8. See Chapter Three, I.
9. It is difficult to say which of the two terms, love or charity, has been the more abused. Perhaps one should say love–charity, or fall back on the Greek *agape*.
10. *Isaiah*, 55.8.
11. I *Corinthians*, 6.19.

II. *John of the Cross, Witness to the Kingdom*

1. *Luke*, 17.24.
2. *ibid.*, 17.23.
3. The Jews claimed that God should be worshipped in Jerusalem, the Samaritans on Mount Garizim. Their antagonism went deep. It was to a Samaritan women that Christ proclaimed an end to the quarrel (*John*, 4.21–24). Concerning the sabbath, cf. *Mark*, 2.27.
4. In 1582 a woman went to him to ask money for a child she accused him of fathering. Knowing that the child was over a

year old, that its mother had never left Granada, and that he himself had been there for less than a year, he told the woman that the child was certainly a miracle.

5. When John lived in a small house near the convent of the Incarnation at Avila, a young girl visited him to try to seduce him. He talked to her, and this meeting was enough to transform her.

6. When he was offered a meal by a stranger passing by, he accepted it although it was a fast day.

7. He dissuaded an officer from abandoning military life to become a religious on the grounds that his life as a soldier was well worth while.

Chapter Six

I. The Body

1. *Ascent*, Book II, chap. 26, par. 8. (Vol. I, p. 197).
2. *Living Flame*, stanza 2, par. 13. (Vol. III, p. 146).
3. *Dark Night*, Book I, chap. 4, *passim*. (Vol. I, pp. 358–63).
4. *Spiritual Canticle*, stanza 12, par. 2. (Vol. II, p. 252).
5. *Ascent*, Book I, chap. 13, par. 6. (Vol. I, p. 61).
6. *ibid.*, Book II, chap. 7, par. 5. (Vol. I, p. 90).
7. *Spiritual Canticle*, stanza 36, par. 5. (Vol. II, p. 381).
8. *Ascent*, Book III, chap. 28, par. 1. (Vol. I, p. 293). 'Of the seven ills into which a man may fall if he set the rejoicing of his will upon moral good'.
9. One could call the Kingdom the presence of God in the world, and the Father, God in himself, the subsistent origin of the incarnate Son.
10. Cf. Chapter Five, I.
11. Gilles Deleuze and Félix Guattari, *Capitalisme et Schizophrénie*, I. *L'Anti–Oedipe*. (Paris, 1972).
12. It might seem to follow from this that the body is waiting for its incarnation. That would not be wrong. The body, though it is itself incarnate, awaits its true incarnation. Death is not the truth of incarnation but the manifestation of it. As the body is not in its truth, but just outside it, the manifestation of the incarnation as such in the body can only destroy it. But we shall see that pain and pleasure can be transformed into one another; suffering and death can only reach this transformation in opposition to death, in Life eternal – in Resurrection.

II. John of the Cross and his Body

1. *Mark*, 2.19–20.
2. Letter to Catalina of Jesus, July, 1581. Letter from Teresa to Gracian, 23 March 1581.

Conclusion

1. *John*, 1.18.
2. *ibid.*, 14.7.
3. Pierre Magnard, *Nature et Histoire dans l'apologétique de Pascal*, (Paris, 1975).
4. *Points of Love*, no. 21. (Vol. III, p. 251).
5. *Living Flame*, stanza 2, par. 36. (Vol. III, p. 160).
6. *Poems*, XX, verse 4. (Vol. II, p. 469).
7. E. Lévinas, *Totalité et Infini*.
8. Dostoievski, *The Idiot*. An exception has to be made of the penultimate scene when Myshkin takes on himself Rogozhin's sin and so restores him to the chance of salvation.

INDEX